Dying

Moira Buffini's plays include *Blavatsky's Tower* (Machine Room), *Gabriel* (Soho Theatre), *Silence* (Birmingham Rep), *Loveplay* (Royal Shakespeare Company), *Dinner* (National Theatre and West End) and *Vampire Story* (NT Connections). She lives in London with her husband and children.

Nikolai Erdman was born in 1902, and began working in the theatre during the period of relative creative freedom which followed the Russian Revolution. He helped to found the Moscow Theatre of Satire in 1924, and Meyerhold directed his first play, *The Mandate*, at his own recently formed theatre in 1925; but *The Suicide* was banned before its dress rehearsal in 1929, and Erdman was exiled to Siberia from 1933 to 1940. He wrote little original work following his rehabilitation, although he joined Yuri Lyubimov at the newly founded Taganka Theatre in 1964. He died in 1970. *The Suicide* was first performed in Britain by the Royal Shakespeare Company in 1979, three years before it received a belated Russian premiere.

MOIRA BUFFINI

Dying For It

a free adaptation of
The Suicide
by Nikolai Erdman

faber and faber

First published in 2007
by Faber and Faber Limited
3 Queen Square, London WC1N 3AU

Typeset by Country Setting, Kingsdown, Kent CT14 8ES
Printed in England by Bookmarque, Croydon, Surrey

A CIP record for this book
is available from the British Library

ISBN 978-0-571-23744-9

2 4 6 8 10 9 7 5 3 1

Acknowledgements

I would like to thank Jenny Worton and
Mike Attenborough for introducing me
to Erdman's play and for the freedom
they gave me to adapt it. I'd like to thank
Kathy Burke for starting the play's journey
towards production, and Anna Mackmin
for completing it. Also Charlotte Pyke
for her invaluable literal translation;
St John Donald and Georgina Lewis; and,
finally, Dinah Wood and Simon Trussler
at Faber for all their help, as ever.

Author's Note

I've been asked to write an author's note
To explain why I don't put all the full stops in.
The text is not poetry
It is drama
It needs to be useful to actors
And I think this is.

Dying For It was first performed at the Almeida Theatre, London, on 8 March 2007. The cast was as follows:

Semyon Semyonovich Podsekalnikov Tom Brooke
Maria Lukianovna, 'Masha' Liz White
Serafima Ilyinichna Susan Brown
Alexander Petrovich Kalabushkin Barnaby Kay
Margarita Ivanovna Peryesvetova Sophie Stanton
Yegor Timoveivich Paul Rider
Aristarkh Dominikovich Grand-Skubik Ronan Vibert
Kleopatra Maximovna, 'Kiki' Michelle Dockery
Father Yelpidy Tony Rohr
Viktor Viktorovich Charlie Condou
Stepan Vasilievich Dominic Charles-Rouse
Oleg Leonidovich Gil Cohen-Alloro

Director Anna Mackmin
Design Lez Brotherston
Lighting Neil Austin
Music Stephen Warbeck
Sound John Leonard
Choreography Scarlett Mackmin
Casting Julia Horam

Characters

Semyon Semyonovich Podsekalnikov
an unemployed man, aged twenty-seven

Maria Lukianovna, 'Masha'
his wife, a worker, aged twenty-five

Serafima Ilyinichna
her mother, a cleaner

Alexander Petrovich Kalabushkin
their neighbour, a fairground stallholder

Margarita Ivanovna Peryesvetova
his lover, owner of a coffee shop

Yegor Timoveivich
a postman

Aristarkh Dominikovich Grand-Skubik
a member of the intelligentsia

Kleopatra Maximovna, 'Kiki'
a romantic

Father Yelpidy
a priest

Viktor Viktorovich
a writer

Stepan Vasilievich
Oleg Leonidovich
undertakers

Two Beggar-Musicians

DYING FOR IT

Russia in the late nineteen-twenties.
An urban slum.

Act One

In the darkness, we hear:

Semyon Masha
Masha
Are you asleep?

There is a sharp intake of breath as Masha starts into wakefulness.

Masha What?

Semyon Shhhh it's just me
Sorry, sorry

Masha Semyon

Masha returns to an exhausted sleep.

Semyon Masha
Are you awake?

Masha Semyon

Semyon Have we got any food left?
I need some black pudding

Masha What?

Semyon Is there any left?

Masha Pardon?

Semyon Did we eat all that black pudding?

Pause.

Masha Did you look?

3

Semyon I thought you might just know
  You served it and
  I thought you might remember

Masha You wake me
  In the middle of the night
  For this?

Semyon I was just asking

Masha Your own feet won't carry you?

Semyon It's cold. I thought if you remembered it would save a wasted journey

Masha How could you?

Semyon Masha

Masha I can't believe you've done this

Semyon I didn't

Masha Not even you

Semyon I'm only hungry

Masha Go to sleep

Semyon Masha

Masha Don't you dare wake me up again

She turns from him. He sighs.

Semyon I won't

We hear them both bitterly try to settle. Pause.

Masha You've killed me with that black pudding, Semyon. I'm not joking; you've destroyed me. I get up at five in the freezing dark. I'm at work at six every day for hour after hour after hour; a mind-numbing, gruelling slog – and when I finally fall into bed, shattered, what d'you do?

4

What d'you do, Semyon?
Are you asleep?

Semyon (*waking*) What?

Masha I was talking to you

Semyon What did you say?

Masha I said just because you're awake chewing the blanket, it doesn't mean I have to be. The least you could do is let me sleep

Semyon But

Masha But no, you wake me up to chat about black pudding

Semyon Is there some left?

Masha Yes, yes, there is
   Yes, there's black pudding
   Because you didn't eat it at teatime

Semyon Don't start, Masha

Masha That's why you're hungry now

Semyon I can't stand / your nagging

Masha Why didn't you eat when it was in front of you? My mother and I go out of our way to put food / on this table

Semyon Yes, and that's the point; / that's the point

Masha We put more food on your plate than / on our own

Semyon Yes, you do, and that's the point –
   You do it to humiliate me

Masha What?

5

Semyon No wonder I can't eat. I'm a parasite. I'm a bloodsucking leech. I haven't got a job; I bring in / no money

Masha Now is not the time for this

Semyon And I eat away at the family resources. You pile my plate like that to rub it in / to demean me –

Masha Don't start, Semyon

Semyon I've got eyes
    I can feel

Masha I can't stand / your self-pity

Semyon You're doing it to punish me. You're killing me with / generosity

Masha I'm killing you?

Semyon That food's like ashes in my mouth. And in the middle of the night when I'm lying in bed starving to death – just the two of us under one blanket and no one to witness – you crucify me with black pudding

Masha I crucify you with black pudding?

Semyon In your own way, yes

Masha Well I'm sorry. (*She is getting out of bed.*) Let it never be said that I crucified my man with black pudding. I'll get you some now. You eat your fill. Let me furnish you, Semyon

> *Masha lights a candle. Her young, open features would look fine if they were better fed and had more sleep. Her nightwear would keep out a polar storm.*

Semyon Can't you see what you're doing to me?

> *Masha holds the candlelight to his pained visage. He too is young: twenty-seven. His hair stands in tufts; he is flushed with stress. His eyes show great sensitivity.*

Masha God in Heaven, this is no way to live
Still, what can you do, eh?

She exits. Semyon lights a candle by the bed.

Semyon No way to live
No way to live

He catches sight of his reflection. It appals him. He turns from the mirror.

I am a maggot, not a man

Masha returns with a half-eaten sausage of black pudding and some bread.

Masha Right; what d'you want it with?
Cold spuds or hard bread?

Semyon Makes no difference 'cause I'm not having any

Masha You what?

Semyon I wouldn't eat it if you buried me up to my neck in it

Masha Oh for God's sake

Semyon Look at you: eyes like a suffering beast. How can I eat food when it's served by an aching martyr?

Masha Why do I even bother?

Semyon You're playing all downtrodden, Masha, when we both know that you're really the man of the house. You bring home the money. It's you that wears the trousers, Masha, isn't it?

Masha Well, I wish I was wearing 'em now 'cause it's freezing out here

Semyon (*indicating his heart*) It's freezing in here, too. You'd squeeze the soul out of me and spread it on that bread, wouldn't you? You think that just because I'm unemployed I'm not a proper man

Masha Do I?

Semyon You think I have no heart, no pride

Masha Is that what I think?

Semyon This life is destroying me

Masha Semyon, you're just hungry

Semyon I fear for myself, Masha. I'm falling apart. Look what's happening to me. I've got a symptom. Look at my symptom

Semyon sits on the edge of the bed, throwing off his blankets. He crosses his legs. He hits his knee with the side of his hand. It jerks up in a reflex action.

Did you see that?

Masha Yes

Semyon It's a fucking symptom. That never used to happen

Masha You might get a job in a circus with that, but it's no way to live

Semyon What do you mean by that?

Masha I mean we can't go on

Semyon Well, let me set you free, Masha
Let me take myself away
Would you rather I cut my throat or hanged myself?

Masha Oh spare me please

Semyon 'Cause that's what you're saying, isn't it?
You wish I was dead

Masha Well, right at this moment / Semyon

8

Semyon And why shouldn't you? You'd be better off without me

Masha I'd be better off without your whingeing, that's for sure

Semyon Well, I won't disappoint you

Masha Good

Semyon My God I won't

Semyon blows out his candle.

Masha What are you doing?

Semyon I always knew you were a hard-faced troll

Semyon blows Masha's candle out. She squeals. The candlestick falls from her hand and breaks. The room is completely dark.

Masha Semyon
Semyon, where are you?
Stop this
Please, whatever I said I'm sorry
I hate the dark

Serafima, Masha's mother, appears standing in the doorway. She is lit by a shaft of moonlight; a woman of no subtlety and indefatigable physical strength.

Serafima Masha, you know I never intrude
You know how careful I am of your private married life
But the walls are like card in here
I should think the whole building's woken to your squawking
What's going on?

Masha Ask my husband

Serafima Are you crying?

Masha (*tearfully*) No

Serafima What's up, Semyon? Let's have it

Masha Semyon?

Serafima Come on, lad, speak up. She's bawling

Masha Senyechka, talk to me

Serafima Are you a stone, Semyon?

Masha Where are you?

Serafima Perhaps he's had a stroke
Or a fit
Maybe his heart's packed in
Or his brain

Masha Oh merciful God
Mother, find the candle

Serafima Where?

Masha I don't know; grope around on the floor

Serafima Grope around, she says

Masha Over there by the chair

Serafima I'm groping, I'm groping

Masha Semyon, please. I didn't mean anything

Serafima What chair? Where?

Masha Talk to me for God's sake

There's a loud crack.

Serafima Ow!

Masha What was that?

Serafima The chair, Masha, my head and the chair

Masha We have to have some light

Serafima Holy merciful mother of God, here it is

Masha Semyon, will you talk to me?

Serafima He's hiding or something
It's his idea of a joke

Serafima lights the candle. Masha looks around, fearfully.

Masha He isn't here. Something terrible is happening

Serafima He's probably fallen back asleep, the big ape

Masha (*pulling back the blanket*) He's gone

Serafima Gone where? What for at this time of night?

Masha Mother
I think he's going to top himself

Serafima What?

Masha He said I was crucifying him
He showed me his symptom

Serafima He never

Masha I said it was no way to live and he's gone

Serafima He's going to what himself?

Masha Top himself
Finish it
End it all
Self-murder

Serafima Oh

Masha Hand me my skirt
I've got to find him
This is a nightmare
Where are my shoes?

Serafima Here are his pants

Masha I don't need his pants

Serafima His pants, Masha
Jesus be praised

Masha What for?

Serafima He won't go far without them. A man without pants is like a blind rat; helpless and reluctant to leave the dark. He'll be lurking around here somewhere

Masha But the state he's in. Where can he be?

Serafima Perhaps he's on the toilet; I don't know

Masha He'll be drinking bleach

Serafima We've got none

Masha Electrics in the bath

Serafima We haven't paid the bill; they cut us off

Masha He'll drown himself

Masha takes the candle from Serafima. She moves through the dismal space. We see it's not a proper room at all. Part of a hallway in a once fine but now semi-derelict house has been curtained off, giving Masha and Semyon their bedroom. Serafima has the only private room on their floor.

It looks like a revolution happened in the building a decade before. It suffered serious damage that has never been repaired. What was once a bourgeois home now houses the very poorest.

Masha is making her way upstairs. We can just see the damaged staircase going up to the next landing, on which there are doors to the bathroom and Alexander's room. The rickety stairs continue up to an attic (where Yegor lives) and disappear down to the kitchen, the basement bedsits and the front door. Masha is on the upper landing. We see her trying a door and pleading.

Masha Semyon, open the door. Talk to me / Semyon. Senyechka

Serafima lights another candle – under an icon of the Virgin.

Serafima Blessed Holy Virgin, I pray for the safety of my son-in-law. Preserve him from this lunacy and bring him on his knees safe before me, where I might blacken both his eyes and break his legs to restore him to your everlasting mercy. Amen

Masha (*calling down*) He's locked the door

Serafima Has he said anything?

Masha No. What if he's dead already?

Serafima I'll kill him

Masha I'm going to wake up Alexander Kalabushkin

Serafima You can't do that

Masha He can break the door down

Serafima Not Alexander Kalabushkin – Masha

Masha Why not?

Serafima He's in deep mourning. The poor man only buried his wife last week

Masha Then he'll understand the meaning of my pain

Serafima I heard him through the ceiling earlier on
  Moaning, roaring with grief

Masha We need a man, Mother. It's as simple as that. I can't break that door down alone

Masha goes to Alexander's door and knocks on it. Serafima starts to make her way up the stairs. When she gets to the bathroom door, she listens at it.

Masha Alexander Kalabushkin
It's me, Masha
I need a man
Comrade, I'm desperate

Alexander (*off*) Take a cold bath

Masha Help me, Alexander.
It's your strong arms I need
I have to break the door down

*The door opens. Margarita appears in a pall of seedy
light: a dishevelled woman, in a yellowing nightie;
once beautiful, now sexy. She is one of life's survivors.*

Margarita Break the door down? You're more of a catch
than I thought, Kalabushkin. There's a little trollop here
who's desperate for your arms

Masha Look, I need a strong man, all right?

Margarita Remarkable behaviour, forcing yourself on a
grieving man

Masha Alexander, I'm in misery, please

Margarita Here we are, innocently talking about his poor
late wife – God rest her soul – when you start threatening
to break down the door

Masha Not this door – what d'you take me for? I'm a
respectable married woman

Margarita So am I, love

Alexander Leave it, Margarita

*Alexander appears. He moves like a bear, with effortless
strength. His humanity is often obscured by his bad
behaviour. He is pulling his braces on over his vest.*

Masha Alexander Kalabushkin
I need a man

Alexander I'm happy to oblige, love, but what about your husband?

Masha My husband has locked himself in the toilet to top himself

Margarita To what himself?

Alexander The stupid fool
  Why didn't you say?

  He barges past Margarita and approaches Serafima at the toilet door.

Serafima Knock this door down and save that idiot boy from himself. Everyone knows how strong you are, Alexander Kalabushkin. I've seen you in your shooting gallery down at the fair, taking aim with your muscles, all taut, like a great big –

Alexander (*knocking*) Come on, pal; are you all right? What're you doing in there?

Margarita Knock it in, then

Alexander Shh

Margarita What are you waiting for?

Serafima A shot

Alexander Has he got a gun?

Serafima I don't know

Alexander It's just if he's got a gun, or even a knife, and I start breaking the door down, he might – (*He mimes.*)

Masha I hadn't thought of that

Alexander We have to be very careful

Masha Should I get the police?

Margarita *and* **Alexander** No!

Alexander Why don't you say something gentle, and while he's distracted I'll – (*He mimes.*)

Masha God bless you, Alexander

Alexander slowly approaches the door followed by Masha, then Serafima, then Margarita. He prepares to break down the door and then gives Masha a nod.

Masha Darling it's me, Mashenka
I love you
Forgive me

Suddenly we hear a chain flushing. The door opens. Yegor Timoveivich comes out in his underwear, carrying a newspaper.

Yegor Can't an innocent communist
Take a dump in the night
Without the fucking cavalry?

He creaks up the stairs to the attic; a small man in his thirties, whose hunched shoulders make him look older.

Masha Sorry, comrade

Yegor I love you too

Masha (*to Serafima*) This is all your fault. You said he was in the toilet

Serafima Where else could he be?

Masha He's gone outside; I knew it
He'll be running over the wasteland
Finding a rope, slinging it over a tree –

Serafima Not without his pants
Here, comrades, are his very pants
And no Russian male would ever hang himself without them

Margarita Have you looked in the kitchen?

Masha No
   The kitchen
   He'll have his head in the oven
   Alexander, help me

Alexander Come on, love
   We'll find him

   Margarita is following Alexander. He stops her.

Are you my shadow or what?

   Alexander and Masha hurry down the stairs.

Margarita Isn't that just like him
   Drinking my comfort all night long and then
   'You my shadow or what?'
   It's like a compulsion with him
   First one woman, then another
   And all of us at arm's length
   No wonder his wife croaked, the poor little bag

Serafima Do I know you?

Margarita No

   *We hear a scream from Masha and a loud thud coming
   from downstairs.*

Serafima He's dead
   That's it
   He's killed himself

Margarita I don't believe it

Serafima Heavenly God in your mercy pull him from the
flames of hell where he surely deserves to burn, Amen

Margarita It never stops, does it?
   The train of horrible events
   Only last week a customer of mine
   Set his own beard on fire

Serafima I feel sick
I want to do something awful

Margarita And one night during the revolution
I was with this lad in a doorway
Celebrating the rise of the masses
When we'd finished
He kissed me
Stepped out into the street
And got his face blown off
It would have been me only I was still sorting out my hosiery
My life's like that
Man in my arms one minute – face blown off the next

Serafima Who are you?

Margarita Never you mind

Alexander appears. Serafima abandons Semyon's pants.

Serafima How did he do it?
Was it gas?
Is he stiff?
Has his skin gone green?

Alexander He wasn't there

Serafima Where's Masha?

Alexander Lying in a faint

Margarita What have you done to her?

Alexander She saw a rat licking her pots out. She screamed and hit her head on the cupboard door. She's knocked herself out

Serafima Mother of God
(*To Margarita*) You look like you're useful with a rat
Come with me and we'll kill the beast

Margarita All right, Grandma. I can see I'm not needed here

Margarita passes Alexander with a bitter look and follows Serafima. A grey dawn is beginning to come through the dirty skylight, casting gloomy light on the stairs. Alexander sits on them. He lights a cigarette.

Alexander Who'd blame anyone for ending it all? We are all worthless dogs

Semyon crawls out from under the bed. He pulls newspaper plugs out of his ears. He goes to the table and picks up the sausage of black pudding. He puts it in his mouth. Alexander sees his silhouette.

Don't do it. Stop!

Semyon (*startled*) Shit on fire!

Alexander Put that thing down

Semyon What thing?

Alexander Drop it, Semyon

Semyon Why?

Alexander You don't have to do this We're all your friends here

Alexander restrains him. Semyon puts the black pudding in his pocket.

Semyon What the fuck are you doing, Kalabushkin? Let me go

Alexander I saw you with it in your mouth

Semyon So what?

Alexander Don't do it, lad. There's always something to live for

Semyon What are you talking about? Let me go

Alexander Those women are chewing their tails over you
  Think of them

Semyon I have been

Alexander Where were you?

Semyon Under the bed with newspaper stuffed in my ears
  I just wanted some peace
  I wanted to think what to do – let me go

Alexander Promise you won't do anything until you've
heard me out

Semyon All right

Alexander I beg you as a friend, Semyon Semyonovich
  Just listen to me

Semyon Talk then, I'm listening

Alexander (*releasing him*) I want your whole attention
  Because what I have to say
  Is very meaningful, all right?
  Sit down. Look

*Semyon sits. Alexander opens a scrappy curtain, casting
sickly light over a dying rubber plant, Semyon's
pathetic belongings on a cluttered table and the rest of
the depressing space. We can see overflowing rubbish
bins in the yard outside.*

Life is beautiful, Semyon

Semyon Right

Alexander Life is a miracle, full of wonder

Semyon What has that got to do with me?

Alexander Everything. You're alive, aren't you?
  Here you are, at the dawn of a brave new age

Age of industry and the working man
Age of medicine and electrics

Semyon Yeah and what kind of age is it when they cut us off because of an unpaid bill?

Alexander Good question

Semyon The fucking Dark Age?

Alexander It's like living in caves, isn't it? I spent three weeks standing in line every day just to get them to adjust that bill – their mistake of course. But it doesn't matter whose mistake it is, we're the ones who suffer and you ask yourself finally, is that what I'm living for?

Semyon Yes

Alexander Some bureaucrat in a heated office saying this regulation, that regulation, and if it's not electrics it's the wording on the licence for my stall or a travel permit – one form after another and finally as the queue stretches on before you through eternity you find you're tired of living

Semyon Yes
Yes

Alexander Tired of fucking living just for that
But
Life is beautiful, comrade

Semyon You know I read that in the paper the other day and I'm sure that they'll retract it soon

Alexander You know what your problem is, Semyon?
You think too much

Semyon I know

Alexander You should get your head down
Dignity of labour and all that
Only time you find a bit of peace is when you're working

21

Semyon I'm unemployed

Alexander Oh it's vicious, isn't it? What a struggle

Semyon It's killing me, I swear it
  Every job I go for
  I stand in line with fifty other men
  Who all look just like me
  And forty-nine of us are turned away
  I have no dignity, no labour, no value at all

Alexander How d'you go on with a life like that?

Semyon I can't believe there's no work in Russia. There is so much to do. Why do they have no work for me?

Alexander Listen, you have to find a purpose, lad. Even if you don't find a job, you must find a purpose

Semyon That's just what I was thinking under the bed. What I need is a vocation, a reason for living, and then, down between the floorboards, my fingers chanced on this. It seems like fate

Alexander What is it?

Semyon I hardly dare tell you. It's a manual for playing the tuba

Alexander The tuba?

Semyon Look: you can learn in only twenty lessons

Alexander (*reading*) 'For the first time Theodor Hugo Schultz, celebrated master of music, shares his knowledge with the masses.'

Semyon I might be wrong but I reckon you could make a mint. It's like a licence to print money, this. If I did twenty concerts a month at five roubles a go, plus tips –

Alexander That's a staggering fortune, isn't it?

Semyon At least. I've got the will, I've got the time, I've got the manual; the only thing missing is the tuba

Alexander So a tuba would give you reason to live?

Semyon I reckon it would, comrade

Alexander That's fantastic
I've convinced you
Life's amazing; a thing of beauty
Now give me the gun

Semyon What gun?

Alexander The gun I saw you putting in your mouth

Semyon Are you making a fool out of me?

Alexander You were trying to top yourself

Semyon To what myself?

Alexander To shoot yourself

Semyon Was I?

Alexander Everybody knows it

Semyon Everybody?

Alexander Yes

Semyon Top myself?

Alexander Yes

Semyon Why?

Alexander Oh, come on, I can't say I blame you
That mother-in-law
How d'you fucking endure it?
And living off Masha
The guilt must be terrible
She's old before her time – knackered
It's shameful

Semyon Who told you all this?

Alexander Masha

Semyon Get out
  Leave me alone

Alexander Now come on, Semyon
  In all the important ways
  Your life is beautiful

Semyon Go to hell

Alexander I will, but give me the gun first

Semyon Are you absolutely mad? Where would I get a
gun?

Alexander Anywhere; they're ten a rouble these days.
Panfidich traded his razor for one at Borzov's round the
corner

Semyon Borzov traded a gun for a razor?

Alexander It didn't have a permit, like. But then, if
you're only going to use it once . . .

  *Semyon is suddenly rifling through the belongings on
  his table.*

What're you doing? Semyon, hand it over

  *Semyon finds a razor. He brandishes it at Alexander,
  who backs away.*

Semyon Swedish steel
  My father's

Alexander What are you doing with that?

Semyon I reckon that maybe
  I'll not be shaving in this world again

Alexander Semyon, I implore you
  To concentrate totally
  On the fact that life is wonderful

Semyon Thanks, Alexander
You've shown me the light
And here's my gun
A pretty tasty way to end it all

Semyon chucks the black pudding at Alexander, then exits out of the window.

Alexander If you wake Borzov at this hour he'll fucking murder you

Semyon (*off*) Save me the bother, then, won't he?

Pause.

Alexander I am a worthless dog

He takes a bite of the black pudding. Serafima and Margarita enter, with the semi-conscious Masha.

Serafima Don't drag her, she's not a sack

Margarita She's bloody heavy

Serafima Get her thighs

Margarita I have

Alexander Give her here

Alexander effortlessly slings Masha over his shoulder.

She doesn't weigh anything;
She's like a little feather bed

He takes her to the bed and puts her on it.

Serafima It was a huge beast, Alexander Kalabushkin; a red-eyed, pestilent, pregnant bitch. We got it with the spud-masher; pulverised its head. Very pleasant chicken flavour, rat

Masha Semyon

Alexander She needs air, poor girl. I'll unbutton her

Margarita *and* **Serafima** I'll do it

Masha Where's my Semyon?
  Is he dead?

Alexander Well not yet, no
  But I have to tell you,
  He's bloody determined

Masha Where is he?

Alexander Gone into the night

Serafima With no pants?

Alexander I tried to stop him but he brandished a razor at me

Masha I have to find him. I was horrible to him. It's my fault

Serafima (*to Alexander*) You should have broken both his legs
  You should have forced him to see reason.
  We should get the police

Alexander *and* **Margarita** No!

Serafima They'd soon prosecute him. And the court would sort him out

Margarita You can't sentence a man to live

Serafima Why not? He deserves it

Margarita What, the ultimate deterrent? The life penalty?

Serafima Who are you?

Margarita Just a stranger, freezing in the night

Masha What's the answer, then? What'll we do with him?

Alexander Get him a tuba

Serafima No

Masha A what?

Alexander A tuba

Margarita It's an instrument. Like a trumpet but bigger

Masha He wants a tuba?

Alexander It'll be his salvation
If he gets a tuba I guarantee
He'll never top himself
His eyes lit up when he spoke of it
He's found a way, you see
Of being independent
He wants to play for money

Masha So how much do these tubas cost?

Margarita About fifty roubles

Masha If we had fifty roubles
My Semyon would never dream
Of taking his own life

Alexander Don't I know it, love

Margarita I've got a tuba

Serafima Well, I've heard it all now, I really have

Margarita If you're not interested –

Alexander Have you not realised who this is?

Margarita Shut it, Kalabushkin

Alexander This is Margarita Ivanovna Peryesvetova

Masha Who?

Serafima Holy saints protect us. Her?

Alexander The very same

Margarita Well, thanks a lot. Grandma here'll see that news gets back to my husband

Alexander Oh come on, Margarita; does he give a toss?

Margarita Of course he gives a toss. He loves me

Alexander He's eighty-three
You have to feed him with a spoon
What's he going to do?
Set his dentures on me?

Serafima You run that coffee shop
That used to be a decent place
I've heard about the way it's gone

Margarita I'm sure you have. It's a successful business now
A rare feat these days

Serafima I've heard that it's a decadent shebeen
A gambling den of smutty dancing girls
With party members, lice and drunken priests

Margarita And instruments for the Federated Socialist Jazz Quintet, including a tuba. Maybe even two

Masha Margarita Ivanovna –

Margarita That is my name

Masha It's a pleasure to meet you
Really
To have a genuine businesswoman in our humble home
It's an honour and an inspiration

Margarita Yes, it must be

Masha Would you take pity on a desperate wife and her poor old senile mother and lend us one of your tubas? We'd do anything

Margarita Well, I was going to suggest a small rental fee but I can see you're a bit hard-pressed. So what I really

need is someone regular to clean my gents' latrines.
Perhaps your mother would oblige?

Masha Mother
This could save us

Serafima You think I'm shy of work?
You think I'm scared of your latrines?
I'm the woman who's cleaned where no one else would
go. I spent fifteen years mopping gore off a bone surgeon's
floor. During the war I put eyes and body parts in sacks –

Masha Thanks, Mother

Margarita The tuba's yours, then. Come and get it

Alexander I'll carry it for you, Masha. Least I can do

Margarita Isn't that nice? You can help her with your
big, strong arms

Alexander (*to Margarita*) You think I'm a total bastard,
don't you?

Margarita (*to Masha*) Men are a burden, always

Margarita exits with Masha and Alexander.

Serafima (*calling after them*) What if he comes back
before you do?
What if he tries something bad?
Hell fire, I feel sick again
His future on earth might depend on me
I know; I'll rinse his pants

Serafima exits upstairs to the toilet.
*Semyon enters through the window. He looks
around, making sure the coast is clear. He takes a
package out of his pocket and unwraps it: a gun. He
puts a couple of bullets in the chamber and closes it.
He puts it down.*
He sits. He furnishes himself with pen and paper.

29

Semyon (*writing*) 'In the event of my death –'

Serafima comes out of the toilet with a dripping pair of pants.

Serafima Semyon, look

Semyon I'm looking

Serafima Your pants. Good as new. Bit of carbolic and a quick scrub

Semyon Could I be alone for a minute, please?

Serafima Wait. I've got a joke for you
You'll die laughing
There were these Germans during the war

Semyon What Germans?

Serafima Just Germans, you know, any Germans

Semyon What about them?

Serafima Well, they ate a live pug. Ha, imagine that

Semyon A what?

Serafima A live pug! My dead husband told me that. Oh, he was funny.
A pug is a dog, Semyon

Semyon They ate a dog?

Serafima Well, people don't eat live dogs

Semyon And?

Serafima And them Germans did

Semyon Serafima

Serafima Never mind, I've got another

Semyon Will you go away?

Serafima You'll love this one; it's a true story
   During the war in our village
   We had a Turk in jail
   A little chap, injured he was; shell-shock
   His head used to shake all the time like this
   We used to go and peep at him – so comical

Semyon I'm busy. Can't you see?

Serafima Anyway, one night we took him bread and meat
   Now this Turk is starving, desperate for food, right?
   But he can't speak Russian so he jumps up
   Arms outstretched when he sees us
   But his head's still shaking, so we say
   'Don't you want it? Don't you want it?'
   And he goes (*She mimes.*)
   So we take it all away again

   Serafima roars with laughter.

Semyon Will you get out?

Serafima Holy Jesus, did we ever laugh about that Turk

Semyon Do I have to lock you in your room?

   *Serafima goes to her room. She turns in the doorway,
   inspired.*

Serafima I know; during the Coronation, this Jew
decided he would chain himself to the palace gates –

   Semyon starts throwing things at Serafima's door.

Semyon OUT

Serafima And when Blessed Alexander caught him, he
said –

Semyon OUT
   OUT

Serafima exits. Semyon returns to the table and sits.

(*Reads.*) 'In the event of my death –'

He continues to write.

'No one is to blame.
Signed, Semyon Semyonovich Podsekalnikov.'

*Semyon puts the gun to his temple and closes his eyes.
He lowers it.*

*He puts the gun in his mouth and closes his eyes. He
lowers it.*

*He puts the gun to his heart. He rocks with despair,
staring hopelessly at the new day.*

Act Two

*The winter afternoon light has managed to find its way
into the space. Semyon is sitting on a stool, holding a
tuba. The manual is in front of him. Masha and Serafima
are watching with anxious interest.*

Semyon *(reads)* 'Chapter One. How to play. The tuba is
played with three fingers. Put the first finger on the first
valve, the second finger on the second valve and the third
finger on the third valve.'

*He looks up, holding his position. He looks handsome,
confident.*

How's that?

Serafima You're a natural

Masha You look amazing

Semyon 'Upon blowing into the mouthpiece, the note
"B" is obtained.'

Semyon blows. He blows again. Nothing.

It's not doing it
  Why isn't it doing it?

Serafima *(to Masha)* Oh Masha, hold on tight.
  If he gives up on this one we're lost

Semyon Hang on, hang on a minute: 'How To Blow.'

Masha You look really gifted
  Really elegant, Semyon, really

Semyon 'In order to blow properly, I, Theodor Hugo

33

Schultz, internationally renowned Concert Tubist, suggest a simple and economical method.

'Tear off a little piece of yesterday's newspaper and place it on the tongue.' Newspaper – we need paper

Serafima and Masha start hunting through the clutter of the room.

Serafima Does it have to be yesterday's?

Semyon No

Masha (*finding one*) Here. Here

Semyon Right. Tear off a bit
A smaller bit than that; do you want to choke me?
Put it on my tongue

Masha does so. Semyon mumbles unintelligibly.

Masha Pardon?

More unintelligible mumbling. Masha looks blank. Semyon spits out the paper.

Semyon I said will you read the next instruction? God!

Semyon puts another piece of paper in his mouth.

Masha 'Tear off a little piece of yesterday's newspaper and place it on the tongue.'

Semyon Uhhhhh

Masha 'Then, spit the paper on to the floor
While spitting, try to memorise the position of your mouth.
Having mastered it, blow, just like you spit.'

Semyon Uhhhhh

Semyon prepares himself. He spits. Without moving his mouth, he puts it over the mouthpiece. He blows. Nothing.

Masha Dear God in Heaven
   If you exist
   Please let him make a sound

   Semyon blows. A loud, shattering bellow from the tuba.

Serafima (*to Masha*) I told you I was right about God. There's your proof

Semyon Masha, hand in your notice. Your working days are over

   Masha embraces him.

Twenty concerts a month at five roubles each plus tips. In pure earnings per year, that's . . . Hang on, I wrote it down. (*He rummages in his pocket.*) 'In the event of my dea –' No! (*He chucks the paper on the desk.*) Here it is. Per year, at least one thousand three hundred and twenty roubles

Serafima But you haven't learnt to play it yet

Semyon Are you deaf?

   He blows the instrument again. A loud bellow.

Masha It's beautiful
   You're brilliant

Semyon Just think, just think, Mashenka, how good it'll be.
   Imagine it, me coming home from a weekend concert
   Applause still ringing in my ears
   Pockets stuffed with money,
   You waiting on our doorstep, dressed in fine cotton prints
   You'll sit me on our chaise-lounge and I'll say
   'Has your mother polished our floors today?'
   And you'll say

35

Masha Yes, Senyechka
   With our polishing machine

Serafima You'd better learn to play it first

Semyon Listen to the music, woman

   He blows another bellowing note. Yegor appears on the stairs.

Yegor What in hell's name is that? *Battleship Potemkin* coming up the street?

Semyon Get used to it, comrade. It's your new neighbour

Yegor You're not playing that in here

Semyon Yes I am

Yegor Over my dead body

Semyon Rather yours than mine, mate

Yegor I'll complain about you
   The housing committee will hear about this
   The rooms are like gold dust, you know

Semyon Shut up

Yegor I'll fill in a form about you

   Semyon blows. Yegor disappears, slamming his door.

Semyon And then I'll say, 'Where's my eggnog?'
   I'll have eggnog with every meal

Masha It's a sin, the way you love eggnog

Semyon And your mother'll bring me one on a tray

Masha In a proper glass

Semyon On a doily. And I'll say, 'Mashenka, is the nursery decorated yet?'

Masha And I'll – (*She is choked.*)
   Oh Senyechka

Serafima Will you learn to play the blasted thing?

Semyon If I'm to develop as a Concert Tubist I need peace, Serafima. These are vital moments of creativity

Masha We'll have a nursery

Semyon Silence and focus, please. (*He reads.*) 'Scales. The scale is the umbilical cord of music. Once you have mastered the scale, you are a born musician.' Well, it can't be that hard

Masha And my fine cotton prints will get bigger and bigger until one day –

Semyon looks at his wife, full of love.

Serafima Will you let him get on with it?

Masha Learn your scales, Senyechka

Semyon turns back to the book. He reads:

Semyon 'In order to conquer the scale, I, Theodor Hugo Schultz, internationally renowned Concert Tubist, suggest the following cheap and easy method. Go out and buy yourself a . . .'

He turns the page.

'Piano.'

Serafima and **Masha** A piano?

Semyon That can't be right
What's he talking about?
(*Reads*) 'Buy yourself a . . .
(*Checks to see if pages are stuck.*) Piano.'

Masha Read on. It can't be right

Semyon 'Check the appendix for more information on the piano.'
Appendix, appendix

(*Reads*) 'Play the scale on your piano according to the diagram below and then copy it to your tuba.'
No, no, it can't be
Mashenka, Serafima
What are we going to buy a piano with?

Masha Oh no

Semyon Theodor Hugo Schultz you villain
You scum

Masha Where will we get a piano?

Semyon is tearing up the manual.

Semyon World-renowned Concert Tubist?
You're a swindling bastard
Cheat and bastard
Bastard
May you and your scales rot in hell

Semyon is raging with grief.

Serafima You can't trust anyone these days

Semyon What has he done to me?
He was my rock of salvation
I could see my future through this tuba

Serafima Never mind. It made a shocking racket anyway

Semyon This is the end
How will we live?

Masha is trying to comfort him.

Masha We'll manage

Serafima We always manage

Masha We can get by on my wages

Serafima Like we always have

Semyon Meaning I don't count!

Masha What else are we to do?

Semyon It's killing me
What about if we break a cup?
Have we got enough to replace it?

He breaks a cup.

No. Can we afford a new plate? NO

He smashes a plate. Yegor Timoveivich comes out of his room to watch.

Masha You BABY

Semyon Can we afford your mother? NO

Serafima I have a job cleaning toilets now

Semyon Why don't I have a job?
What about if I smash this vase?

Masha That's mine
It's mine

Semyon Can we buy another on your shitty wage?

Serafima *(to Masha)* Say we can't!

Masha Semyon, don't!

They fight for the vase. Semyon smashes it. Masha lets out a howl.

Serafima Now look what you've done

Masha That was mine
I made it at school
When I was a little girl
When I still had hope
And now you've ruined it

Semyon Just like I've ruined you; that's what you're saying

Masha Stop telling me what I'm saying

Semyon I wish this was my skull

Semyon smashes another plate.

Masha You want to smash things? Let's smash them.
Can we afford a new mirror? – NO

Masha smashes the mirror. Semyon is shocked.

Semyon What are you doing? That's seven years' bad luck

Masha Everything shattered
Plates, cups
My human life
And you don't care

Masha is sobbing. Semyon is completely taken aback.

Semyon Mashenka
Since the day we married I've let you down
You'd be much better off without me
You should leave. I beg you
For God's sake leave me
I'll disappear

Masha You'll what?

Semyon I'll vanish
Blow away like a smokewreath
Extinguish myself

Masha How dare you say that
Me and my mother
We are the only two people in the world
Who would stand by your grave and weep for you
You go ahead and top yourself
But know this: I won't be there and neither will she
Do it and you die alone.
You're a selfish bastard, Semyon

Pause.

Serafima Are you leaving him, then?

Semyon and Masha are both devastated.

Is she leaving you, Semyon? Is that the plan?
(*To Masha.*) We could go back to the village
The bone surgeon wouldn't let me starve
And there's work digging turnips out of the frost
Come on now
Come on

Serafima escorts Masha into her room. She closes the door. Yegor exits. Semyon is alone.

Semyon Plates, cups, my human life
Two people standing over the grave
Only one who cares if I live or die
And I have shattered her
Set her free
Let's have one less flea in the fleapit
Split me with a fingernail and wipe me away

He grabs his gun.

Count to ten and the torment's over

*He puts the gun to his temple and closes his eyes.
Alexander enters, leading Aristarkh Dominikovich
Grand-Skubik up the stairs. His ragged suit and coat
still show signs of impeccable tailoring. He's in his
forties, highly educated and quite desperate.*

Semyon One, two, three –

Alexander He lives up there

Aristarkh I can't thank you enough

Semyon Four, five

Alexander The small fee we talked about then, for
arranging the meeting –

Semyon Six –

Aristarkh Of course

Semyon Seven –

Aristarkh That should cover it

Semyon Eight, nine –

Alexander Give him a shout; he hasn't got a bell

Alexander exits back down the stairs.

Semyon Ten

Aristarkh (*calling*) I say, comrade

Semyon is utterly startled. He hides the gun and draws back the curtain.

Sorry to interrupt. I hope you weren't busy. Do carry on

Semyon You're fine

Aristarkh Well, I shan't keep you for long. Do I have the honour of addressing Semyon Semyonovich Podsekalnikov?

Semyon Yes, sir

Aristarkh Oh, don't call me 'sir'. Here we are, two ordinary thinking chaps, no difference between us

Semyon Right

Aristarkh Are you the same Podsekalnikov who has declared an intention to kill himself?

Semyon Who told you that? I mean no, I never said that. I'm not him. I've got no weapons here

Aristarkh Well, I was taking my coffee at Margarita Ivanovna's – as is my habit, being a keen observer of the proletariat – and it was the topic of all the conversation

Semyon No way

Aristarkh That fairground chap Kalabushkin had us all enthralled. You pulled a razor on a him; good for you; shows a fine spirit

Semyon Look, if you're looking for unlicensed firearms I can't help you. And I don't know anything about anyone trying to top themselves

Aristarkh Ah. (*He picks up Semyon's discarded note from the table and reads.*) 'In the event of my death, no one is to blame.' Well, this is interesting, you see, because it looks like a suicide note. And then you've signed it, haven't you?

Semyon I haven't done anything wrong, sir

Aristarkh My dear equal, I haven't come here to persecute; on the contrary; I'm here to assist you

Semyon How?

Aristarkh Well, my first duty is obviously to try and persuade you not to do it. But if you are determined then I think you should know that this note shows some very wrong thinking. Are you determined?

Semyon slowly nods.

Aristarkh Well then. This note is based on an entirely faulty point of view

Semyon What do you mean?

Aristarkh Semyon – I may call you Semyon, mayn't I, in these egalitarian days?

Semyon Yes

Aristarkh I have bolted down my coffee, so keen was my desire to meet you

Semyon Why?

Aristarkh Because you are shooting yourself. You have an opportunity here that cannot be wasted. It is wonderful

Semyon Is it?

Aristarkh But you must shoot yourself not just as an individual, you must shoot yourself as a responsible member of society. Remember, you are not alone. You are one of us; you're a thinking man. So think, Semyon, think. Why is this a useless note?

Semyon Er –

Aristarkh No one is to blame? Poppycock; of course someone is to blame. Look around you, Semyon; what do you see?

Semyon Not much

Aristarkh Russia. You see Russia. Look at her finest men; the intelligentsia. What do you hear?

Semyon Nothing

Aristarkh Precisely; because they have been silenced, silenced like white slaves in the proletariat's harem. Semyon, you are in a position of great power

Semyon Am I?

Aristarkh You are a dead man

Semyon Well, not yet –

Aristarkh You soon will be. And nowadays, only the dead may say what the living think. I come to you as to a dead comrade. I come to you on behalf of Russia's thinking men

Semyon I'm not anyone important, sir

Aristarkh You could be. My dear boy, you're right to take leave of your life. It's not worth living; of course it's

not; it must be simply ghastly. But someone is to blame.
I cannot speak without restraint but you can. You have
nothing to lose, nothing to fear. You are soon to be free.
And so, Semyon, tell me, who do you blame?

Semyon Who do I blame?

Aristarkh Don't be afraid, hold nothing back

Semyon Theodor Hugo Schultz

Aristarkh Well, I don't know him personally but I'm sure
the Comintern is full of chaps just like him. So let's blame
them all, shall we?

Semyon What?

Aristarkh My dear fellow, I'm afraid you still don't
understand why you are killing yourself. Allow me to
explain

Semyon Go on

Aristarkh You want to die for the truth, don't you?

Semyon Yes

Aristarkh And what is the truth?

Semyon I don't know

Aristarkh The circumstances of your life
   The grinding poverty, your unemployment
   Have led you to despair
   Now these circumstances are a result
   Of certain political and economical factors.
   Who controls these factors?
   Come on, Semyon, spit it out
   (*Prompting him*) The g . . .
   The gov . . .

Semyon The government?

Aristarkh Just to hear you say it sends a thrill right down my spine. Semyon, I can see the intelligence shining in your eyes. I know you want to die a meaningful, heroic death

Semyon That does sound good

Aristarkh It is good; a more magnificent death could not be found. But you must act quickly. Tear up this useless note and write another. Accuse them, blame them, speak your heart

Semyon Blame the government?

Aristarkh Yes – and defend us, the intelligentsia. And end by asking them the ultimate question: why has a loyal and sensitive citizen like Aristarkh Dominikovich Grand-Skubik not been employed in the construction of humane socialism?

Semyon Who?

Aristarkh Aristarkh Dominikovich Grand-Skubik
That's me
Sorry, didn't I say?

Semyon You'll have to spell it for me

Aristarkh writes it down.

You are not employed either, sir?

Aristarkh Not in the way I would wish. Semyon, when you have written this note, I will personally ensure that the bullet you shoot through your brain will be heard through all Russia

Semyon But why would anyone be interested in me?

Aristarkh Because you will have spoken!

Semyon That simple?

Aristarkh Speak and you're a hero. Men like me will honour you. Your name will become a slogan. I'll make sure that a portrait of your corpse – providing it's not too disfigured – will be on every front page. Russia's intelligentsia will gather round your coffin. Your hearse will be drowning in erudite tokens of respect

Semyon What a death

Aristarkh I would have such a death myself only, alas, I'm needed alive. So, are we agreed?

Semyon A useful, courageous, meaningful death

Aristarkh You need to compose your new suicide note, along the lines that I've suggested. Better still, I could write it – then you have only to sign your name and shoot yourself

Semyon I'll write it myself, sir, if you don't mind

Aristarkh And shall we arrange a time?

Semyon A time?

Aristarkh Would tonight at midnight suit you?

Semyon Oh

Aristarkh You are a true Russian hero and you are my equal. In the name of the intelligentsia, allow me to embrace you
     I find myself overcome
     I didn't cry when my mother died
     Oh, my poor mother
     But now
     Now

   Aristarkh sobs. Semyon comforts him.

Until midnight

   Aristarkh exits, deeply moved.

47

Semyon My name will be remembered
  My life will have meant something
  I'll give them the truth all right
  They will have my truth in buckets
  I will pour my blame all over Russia
  I need paper

  *Serafima and Masha enter from Serafima's room. They
  are dressed to go out.*

Where are you going?

Masha Never you mind

Semyon Are you leaving me?

Masha None of your business

Semyon Well, if you come back, will you bring me some
paper?

Masha Get your own

  They exit down the stairs. Semyon shouts after her.

Semyon It's not just the government, it's you!

  The door slams.

My death will teach her to respect me
  She will realise who she married then
  My death will show them all my mettle
  I am not a maggot. I am not a flea
  And I am not alone

  *Alexander appears at the window with Kleopatra
  Maximovna, a striking young woman dressed in
  bohemian style. She is flushed with anticipation.*

Alexander Semyon –

Semyon (*opening the window*) Have you got any paper,
comrade?

48

Alexander Paper? Waste of time. Got someone here who wants to meet you

Kleopatra Hello

Alexander Come on, girl, have a leg up

Kleopatra Are you Semyon Semyonovich?

Pause. Semyon is gazing at her.

Alexander Well, answer her, lad

Semyon *Oui*

Alexander lifts Kleopatra through the window.

Kleopatra I asked for a clandestine meeting

Semyon *C'est moi*

Alexander Kiki, the small fee I mentioned?

Kleopatra Oh yes. This should cover it

Alexander Clandestine is extra

Kleopatra (*reluctantly giving him some coins*) Outrageous

Semyon What are you doing, Alexander?

Alexander What a friend should

He goes.

Kleopatra I'm Kleopatra Maximovna
But people call me Kiki

Semyon *Bonjour*, then

Kleopatra I've heard about what you're going to do

Semyon Have you?

Kleopatra Are you fully committed? To die at your own hand?

Semyon Yes

49

Kleopatra How can you be so tragic and so brave? I have to beg you, I implore you, do not throw away your beautiful life

Semyon Kiki –

Kleopatra I plead upon my knees
I understand how you must be feeling

Semyon Do you?

Kleopatra Yours is not the only heart to succumb to pain. My own breast is a victim of it too. We are similar, Comrade Potsen . . . Podsek . . .

Semyon Podsekalnikov. Semyon

Kleopatra Semyon, my own breast burns with scorching flames
And sometimes the heat of my emotion is so raw
That I find myself crying out in solitary pain
With no one to hear me but an imaginary love,
'Now, now, end it all
I can't bear living with a heart this full.'
I'm a Romantic, you see

Semyon That's nice

Kleopatra And when I heard what you were doing – killing yourself in your youthful prime – I knew you must be a man of huge sensitivity. Are you a man of great soul?

Semyon Yes

Kleopatra I knew it. Men look at me and they just see a face, they see Kleopatra Maximovna; face, face, face, and when they pursue me they just want my body, they want to take my body and make love to it like a senseless thing, as if my body was just a body alone without a thinking, feeling soul, but Semyon, you wouldn't be like that, would you?

Semyon No

*During the following, Yegor leaves his room in his
postman's uniform. He walks down the stairs,
watching the scene.*

Kleopatra I've been a prisoner of my body all my life.
I knew I was in trouble at fifteen, when my mother took
me to buy shoes and the shop owner lost control of
himself. The sight of my stockinged foot was too much
for him and he sunk his teeth into my toe. It was just a
little bite really, but my mother thought I had provoked
him and she sent me away. From then I have limped from
one man to another. There was my airplane pilot who
said, 'Your body is my sun and my moon and without it,
I am without light,' and when I left him he flew his plane
over the city in spirals crying my name; then there was
my communist who said my body was his Supreme Soviet
– but he was nothing but a penile imperialist, and when I
abandoned him he cursed me and left the Party; then
there was the writer who called me his perfect muse and
then said I drove him distracted; but none of them, none
of them has ever truly found me, or owned me or even
come close. All my life I've searched for the man who
would understand my soul and now I think I've found
him, found him in you, and it's too late – you are to die
in this cruel way. You are to kill yourself

Semyon Yes
    But
    Maybe not yet

Kleopatra Semyon, I've come here to plead. You must
end your life only for the purest of reasons
    Listen to the turmoil in your soul. What is it telling you?

Semyon Er –

Kleopatra Look at my eyes. Take my hands. You're an
aesthete, a prince of emotion. Don't resist, let the pain
flow out of you

51

Semyon Right

Kleopatra Love is agony

Semyon Yes

Kleopatra Can you feel it? Here?

Semyon Yes

Kleopatra I knew it. You feel it. Don't kiss me – you're too pure

Semyon Sorry

Kleopatra Semyon, angel, I have only one favour to ask: if you are truly determined on this course of action – and how I revere you for it – then kill yourself for the one woman who appreciates the beauty of your soul. Kill yourself for Kleopatra, for Kiki and for love. I'll make a fool of myself at your funeral. My body will be useless for any other man. This is an age when love is despised; when it is trampled. How your death will change that. I will lead Russia's women as they sob upon your grave. We will carry your coffin on our fragrant shoulders. It will be you scorched on my heart for eternity, you I shall cherish to my grave. My remembrance will make you one of Russia's great lovers

Semyon notices Yegor.

Semyon Can't you see this meeting is clandestine?

Yegor You lucky sod

Semyon Is nothing private in this house?

Yegor This stairwell is a public thoroughfare

Semyon I'm asking you nicely to leave

Yegor And I am exercising my right / as a resident –

Semyon Get out –

Yegor As a resident and as a citizen / to be here

Semyon is rummaging for his gun.

Semyon Yegor Timoveivich, I am armed and desperate and I don't care what I do

Yegor You can't threaten me. My mettle was tested in the workers' civil war for freedom

Semyon shakily points the gun at Yegor.

Semyon Please go away

Yegor Have you got a permit for that?

Semyon Sod off, you nosy bastard!

Yegor runs downstairs and exits. Meanwhile, Kleopatra is swooning at the sight of the gun.

Kleopatra Semyon, I'm overcome. Hold me

Semyon Kiki, hang on

Kleopatra Listen to your heart

Semyon I am. But I'm not free –

Kleopatra We are both in chains

Kleopatra kisses him. He is dazzled.

Semyon What do I have to do?

Kleopatra I need your note. Write down the way you feel. I must have it in writing. Mention my name several times. Say you were overwhelmed – because you are overwhelmed, aren't you?

Semyon Yes

Kleopatra Say you despaired of ever being worthy. And then, after your death, my inconsolable grief will move a nation and your name, Semyon Semyonovich Paster . . .

Semyon Podsekalnikov

Kleopatra Yes – will never be forgotten

We hear Masha calling from downstairs.

Masha Semyon? Semyon

Semyon Shit on fire

Kleopatra What is it?

Semyon My
Oh God
It's the cook

Kleopatra The cook?

Semyon Quick –

Masha Semyon?

Semyon (*to Masha*) Get down to the kitchen and make
me some soup

Masha What?

Semyon I said make me some soup
And an eggnog

Masha Who do you think you're talking to?
I'm not your dog
Or your slave
You ungrateful bum

Semyon Quick

Masha After everything I said
To talk to me like that?
You pathetic turd

Kleopatra What an uncouth person

Masha I was all for getting straight on a train, but my
mother said we should give you one more chance

Semyon She sometimes brings her mother, who is vicious and a hag

Semyon is taking Kleopatra up to the landing.

Kleopatra Let's defy her with our love. Kiss me

Semyon No – look – please hide
Just for a minute
I'll get rid of her

We hear Masha calling down the street.

Masha (*off*) Mother, he's still here
He hasn't done it yet – worst luck

Kleopatra Where are you taking me, Semyon?
To your bedroom?

Semyon No

Kleopatra Oh, I am weak
My body is so weak

Semyon Best go in the toilet then

Kleopatra No, don't make me
I'm scared of toilets
I'm too sensitive

Semyon Well, go in there then – quick

He bundles Kleopatra into Alexander's room. She is barely out of sight when Masha appears with Serafima.

Masha (*to Semyon*) What are you doing up there?

Semyon (*grabbing his pants from the balcony*) Pants!

Serafima Prepare yourself, son

Semyon What for?

Serafima This is our last act of kindness towards you
Come on up, Father Yelpidy

Father Yelpidy enters: a man steeped in bitterness and alcohol. His thoughts, at this time of day, are usually as black as his robes.

Semyon Oh, hairy Mary
I don't believe it

Yelpidy I hear you're contemplating a mortal sin, boy

Semyon Listen, Father,
I don't believe in God

Yelpidy Well, believe in Him or not, He has no forgiveness for those who despair

Semyon Then why did he create a world like this?

Yelpidy He didn't. He gave us the Garden of Eden. We created this world through our own sinning natures

Semyon Masha, I can't believe you've brought him here

Masha I'm clutching at straws

Semyon How could you do it?

Masha Where else can I turn, Semyon?

Yelpidy You don't believe in God; that's fine. But think of the horrible shock when you wake in your coffin and instead of rising up to Heaven your soul is pulled by clawing demons down to the murk of Hell. That'll be the moment that you realise He exists – when it's too late and He's abandoned you. Because, believe me, if you take your own life that is what will happen

Semyon Great

Serafima Watch your language in front of the priest, you dirty little boy

Alexander enters. On his way up to his room, he stops to listen. He is amused.

Yelpidy Let me tell you, you'll suffer agonies so extreme they cannot be described. Imagine all your extremities being slowly fried while demons blow poison in your ears. Imagine the pain as it scalds and eats your brain. Imagine them peeling your blistered skin off and bursting your eyeballs with skewers. Imagine them raping you over and over with hot metal implements of every kind

Semyon Oh for God's sake

Yelpidy Yes, for God's sake! For God's sake it'll happen, for you are committing the foulest sin

Semyon Will you get him out of here?

Serafima He hasn't had his tea yet
He's not going until he's had his tea

Yelpidy And do you have a little biscuit, Serafima Ilyinichna?

Serafima I'll find you something tasty, Father

She runs down to the kitchen. Alexander is at his door.

Semyon Alexander
Don't go in there

Alexander Why not?

Semyon Stay down here
Join in the fun

Alexander No ta

Semyon Wait – you're a sinner too. You're far worse than me. He can save us as a job lot

Alexander I'm a Marxist

Semyon So?

Alexander Fuck off

He exits into his room. We hear Kleopatra squeal.

Masha Who's up there?

Semyon Mice

Yelpidy Have you listened to anything I have said?

Semyon Yes. You're enough to make anyone top themselves

Yelpidy God hears your insolence
  He hears all in these godless times
  And he is storing up his vengeance

Masha Father, is there a different tack you could try?

  Yelpidy sighs. He sits.

Yelpidy I should be used to ridicule and rejection by now but it always stings. I spread my pearls before swine every day and no one listens any more. Why do I bother? Why?

Semyon I don't mean to be rude, Father, but I don't believe in God

Yelpidy Then abandon hope. Kill yourself

Masha Pardon?

Yelpidy Go on ahead. Slice your throat, shoot yourself, throw a rope from that landing there and swing from it

Semyon Right
  Well, thanks

Yelpidy Nothing I can do with a godforsaken suicide
  (*He is suddenly inspired.*) Except
  Will you be writing a note, boy?

Semyon Yes

Yelpidy Will you be mentioning despair?

Semyon Don't know yet. Maybe

Yelpidy Then give it to me. Let me read it to the people. Tell them how you turned your back on God. Say how I, Father Yelpidy, begged you to hear His word and save yourself. Tell them how you pushed me away. Then drink poison, blow your head off, drown yourself

Masha Father, what are you saying?

Yelpidy No other sermon I could preach would have more power
    To turn the wayward millions back to God
    The lesson of your terrible despair
    The vision of your empty, godless universe
    Will freeze men's hearts. Their terror
    At your fate will rip desperate prayers
    From out their mouths, like screams. Your suicide
    Desolate boy, will fill my church
    And I, Yelpidy, will gather my new flock
    And nurture them within these humble robes

Semyon So if I kill myself I'm doing it for God?

Yelpidy He works in magnificent and enigmatic ways
    Write your sad defiance down
    And sign it with your wretched name.
    Your lost soul might save ten thousand others

Serafima enters.

Serafima Father, I poked around and found a little bit of meat. I know you'd rather have a biscuit but it's chicken-style stew

Yelpidy You needn't go to trouble over me

Serafima I've also got a little bit of this

She holds up a flask of vodka.

Yelpidy The feast at Cana

Serafima Come on down

Yelpidy Think upon my words, young man. Repent and turn to God – or write that note

Yelpidy exits with Serafima.

Masha I thought he'd speak more kindly
But he hasn't a drink yet I suppose

Semyon What are you trying to do to me?

Masha I'm trying to save your life

Semyon Well, don't bother

Masha I won't

Masha starts putting a few of her pathetic belongings in a bag. There are not many.

Semyon Are you going, then?

Masha Not hanging round here to be the weeping widow

Masha's bag is ready. She shuts it.

Semyon Good luck, then

Masha Thank you

Neither of them can move. They are verging on reconciliation.

Semyon Mashenka

Masha Yes?

Semyon I –

Masha Semyon

Semyon I –

Margarita (*entering*) Sorry to disturb you little turtle doves, but is Alexander Kalabushkin here?

Semyon No, he's not

Masha (*puzzled*) Yes, he is

Semyon No, he's not
  He just went out

Masha No, he didn't

Margarita I see. Who's he up there with?

Semyon No one
  No one, honest

> *Alexander's door opens. We see him with Kleopatra in the doorway.*

Kleopatra You barbarian

Alexander Take a cold bath, love

Kleopatra You savage. Your room smells like the cage of a beast. There's vodka on your breath
  Your hands
  Are huge

Alexander I'm here later on if you want to get close

Kleopatra Animal

> *Kleopatra runs downstairs. Alexander stays on his doorstep quietly laughing. He lights a cigarette. The sun is now setting.*

Semyon, how could you force me to hide in there?

Semyon Kiki

Margarita (*directly beneath Alexander*) What slut are you chasing now?

Alexander There's only one slut for me, Margarita

> *He winks at her and returns to his room, leaving the door open. Kleopatra throws her arms around Semyon, who is mortified.*

Kleopatra He is a blot on the world
  And you, you are the bravest man I've ever met
  I'll revere you for ever

Semyon That's great, Kiki

Kleopatra Remember my note

  She releases him. Masha is disgusted.

Masha 'Kiki'?

Kleopatra Is this your cook?

Semyon Er –

Kleopatra You should get her to sweep up. There's a lot
of broken crockery around. *Adieu*

  She blows him a kiss and leaves.

Masha Your cook?

Semyon Well –

  Masha slaps him round the face.

Masha Useless lying pig

  *She thumps him, then shoves him over. She storms up
  the stairs. She locks herself in the bathroom.*

Margarita Semyon Semyonovich

Semyon Go away

Margarita Come on now
  It's just a little marital
  It won't last

Semyon I know
  I'll be dead

  Semyon starts to cry.

Margarita Are you serious?

Margarita puts her arms around him and comforts him.

Oh come on, love, pick yourself up

Yegor enters. He slowly walks up to his room, watching and listening.

I've thought about ending it from time to time
When it just seems stupid going on
But I haven't got a bone in my whole body
That could harm itself.
You need to dig into adversity and grip it till it squeals
Because in doing that
You'll find out how strong you really are

Semyon I want to make a difference in a way I can't alive

Margarita Has Kalabushkin got you in this state with all his visitors?

Semyon I never want to see the dawn on another day. Come midnight – bang

Margarita is shocked. Alexander has wandered out of his room again.

Alexander (*to Yegor*) Have you no shame? Give him some privacy

Yegor This is a public stairwell

Alexander You're like a little rat, you
Peering out of corners at other people's lives
Haven't you got one of your own?

Yegor Course I have. I live for the struggle

Alexander Piss off

Yegor runs up to his room. Alexander now watches the scene. Semyon is drying his eyes.

63

Margarita Well, if you're that set on it there's nothing
I can say.
You'll be an ideological corpse all right, Semyon
And a very cute one
If you don't mind my saying

Semyon At least I'll be a corpse
That's the main thing

Margarita Well, what do you want to do, then?
If this is going to be your last night on Earth
We'd better make it special.
What d'you fancy?

Semyon Don't know

Margarita You tell Margarita
What would you like to do?

Semyon Have a laugh?

Margarita We'd better throw a party then
To see you on your way
Least they can do is raise you a glass
Hold off till midnight, yeah?
And who knows
You might wake up hungover in the morning
And decide that life's all right

*Semyon nods. Margarita gets up. She notices
Alexander.*

Give Alexander Kalabushkin, a message from me
Tell him he's a goat and a pornographer
And a lumpen, savage beast
Tell him he's a worthless dog
And he's to come and help me carry all the booze

*Alexander goes into his room. Yegor, seeing the coast
is clear, immediately comes out of his room. He creeps
down the stairs, watching.*

You've a face like an icon, Semyon
    It seems a shocking waste

Margarita kisses Semyon; a long kiss.

Midnight

She exits. Yegor tries the bathroom door.

Semyon The zero hour
    Between day and night
    On the strike of twelve
    On the final tock of the final tick
    I'll leave through a gap into –

*Semyon looks up to see Yegor peering through the
keyhole.*

Hey, pervert
    That's my wife in there

Yegor Semyon Semyonovich
    I am looking through this keyhole from a Marxist
point of view
    There is nothing perverted about it

Masha comes out.

Masha Yegor Timoveivich, do you see any worth in me?
    Any value or beauty?

Yegor Maria Lukianovna, you are so lovely
    You are such a proper fine young woman
    That when I pass you on the stairs
    I often find myself looking away
    Glancing aside in case I am dazzled
    And occasionally when you smile at me
    Or make a kind remark –
    As you did when I got my People's Award
    For Speed and Diligence in Postal Deliveries –
    I find I am so moved I have to shut my eyes and breathe

Semyon Unbelievable

Yegor And the only way forward, then, is to see you from a Marxist point of view – when suddenly, you're safely drab and sexless

Masha Thank you, Yegor
I'm going to the station now
Would you ask my husband to pass me my coat?

Yegor Your wife would like her coat, comrade

Yegor hovers in the bathroom doorway, watching the scene. Semyon gets Masha's coat. She walks to him.

Masha (*to Semyon*) Are you going to stop me?

Semyon It's up to you

Semyon holds the coat out for her. Masha puts it on. Their eyes are locked throughout the following exchange.

Yegor That unlicensed gun you pointed at me, comrade

Semyon What about it? You going to fill in a form?

Yegor Are you going to shoot yourself with it?

Semyon I'm a man who doesn't care

Yegor Well, I hope you're doing the decent thing

Semyon What decent thing?

Alexander enters.

Yegor You've got to do it for the Party. The Party needs you. People are losing their fervour now we're not in active revolution any more. There's something in the air, a sense of – I don't know – (*He whispers.*) Disillusionment

Alexander (*to Yegor*) If you want to talk to him, you come through me, all right? You want to enter the lottery for his fate? It'll cost you five roubles

Yegor Do it for the Party, Semyon. You owe them everything

Yegor, threatened, goes into the toilet and locks the door. Semyon and Masha are still staring at each other.

Semyon You don't believe I'll do it, do you? You don't think I'm man enough

Masha Goodbye

Masha leaves. The light is beginning to fade into dusk.

Alexander Call her back

Semyon hangs his head. Alexander comes downstairs.

I reckon that means you're serious.
    You'd better have this, then

He puts a handful of banknotes into Semyon's hand.

Semyon What's this?

Alexander About twenty roubles. Least I can do, mate

Semyon Where did you get it?

Alexander Five roubles for a personal meeting –
clandestine extra – and three for a written suggested cause

Semyon What?

Alexander Here are your written suggested causes. This is from Pugachev the butcher: 'Do it for meat'

Semyon What's going on?

Alexander Here's one from Raisa Filipovna – great stomach on her. Biceps like a poster girl

Semyon Who are these people?

Alexander She says, 'Semyon Semyonovich, bla bla bla . . . sacrifice yourself for the sexual emancipation of all

Russian women . . .' (*Handing the letter to Semyon.*) If you fancy it

Semyon What are you talking about?

Alexander (*looking at the next*) Viktor Viktorovich – he's a writer. He's actually paid to meet you but I haven't fitted him in yet. He goes on and on and on about samovars and troikas and broken guitar strings. Basically, he hasn't got a cause; he just wants to write about you once you're dead. Look through the rest at your leisure

Alexander hands the rest of the letters to Semyon.

Semyon What is all this money for?

Alexander Whatever you like. It's poverty that's bought you to this. So I thought I'd alleviate your poverty

Semyon is moved.

Semyon Thank you, comrade, but
I've no use for it

Alexander is disappointed.

Alexander Have it anyway

Semyon You really did this for me?

Alexander I took a massive cut, obviously

Semyon People really paid you?

Alexander Yes

Semyon Like I'm somebody important?

Alexander Well, you are. You're a fucking hero to them. Nice idea of Margarita's, throwing you a party. You've got to hand it to her, haven't you? She's a classy tart

Semyon You're a pornographer

Alexander And a goat. I'll go and help her with the booze

*Alexander moves away. Semyon opens one of the
notes. He reads.*

Semyon 'Comrade Podsekalnikov
Shoot and your soul flies out of its cage
Like a wild bird on the wind.
Hosanna, it will cry; hosanna . . .'

Alexander (*stopping*) Oh yes, I didn't charge him
I didn't feel I could
He's got no legs
Or fingers
And he's blind
I had to write it down for him

Alexander exits.

Semyon (*reads*) 'God calls to you, like he calls to all
The lost and those tormented in the mind
Break the bonds of pain that hold you here
We will exalt you
Hosanna
We are the only voice of truth on Russia's streets
Do it for us, your brethren in the gutter
Do it for the beggars
And the mad.'

*Semyon stands alone in the fading light.
    He stares into the darkness, a look of determination
growing on his face.*

Midnight.

Act Three

Guests have assembled in Semyon's dingy living space: Margarita, Serafima, Alexander, Aristarkh, Kleopatra and Father Yelpidy. Semyon has been covered in streamers and confetti. Everyone is singing. Two Beggar-Musicians play. Candlelight and gas lamps light the scene. Huge shadows.

All To us has come our very own
  Semyon Semyonovich
  Dear Semyon, Semyon,
  Semyon, Semyon, Semyon
  Drink, drink, drink, drink
  Semyon drink it up

  Margarita hands Semyon one of his last remaining cups, filled with wine.

  Drink, drink, drink, drink, Semyon drink it up!

  Semyon drains the cup.

Semyon Can I afford to replace it? Who cares?

  He smashes it. The guests cheer wildly.

Kleopatra What a man

Aristarkh Such proletarian passion

Alexander You're a fucking hero, Semyon

Serafima That's why we all love you, darling. Father Yelpidy has explained why you're doing what you're doing and I must say I'm impressed. I never thought you had such strong religious feeling in you

Yelpidy (*to Kleopatra*) Have you heard the one about the monk in the bath house?

Kleopatra Don't talk to me about monks. I don't like smut

Yelpidy Ah go on, you do

Semyon gives the Beggar-Musicians a handful of notes. Alexander notices. It troubles him.

Semyon Thanks for that, lads. You keep playing

They do so.

Serafima It's only a pity my fool of a daughter isn't here to support you. I ran to the station looking for her but she was gone. And it's the first opportunity you've ever given her to be proud of you

Semyon turns away.

Yelpidy I just want to say, brethren, comrades, this young man's death will have an impact on every Russian

Aristarkh You are quite correct. Semyon Semyonovich is a catalyst

Serafima Don't be disgusting

Yelpidy Here's to him

Alexander Speech! Speech! Tell them how you're feeling, Semyon. And tell them whose note you're going to run with

Aristarkh The note is not the important thing

Kleopatra Speech!

The other guests join in, calling Semyon to speak. Semyon falters. Pause.

Semyon What time is it?

Aristarkh Ten to midnight

Margarita It's nowhere near. You've got all the time in the world

Yegor enters. He is followed by Viktor Viktorovich, an intense, defensive poet in his early thirties. Semyon seizes his entrance with relief.

Semyon Well, look who's here!
To us has come our very own
Yegor Oh-what's-his-name?

The Beggar-Musicians start to play. Alexander joins in, singing.

Alexander Dear Yegor, Yegor
Yegor, Yegor, Yegor
Drink, drink, drink, drink
Yegor drink it up

Margarita hands Yegor a bottle. He drinks.

All Drink, drink, drink, drink, Yegor drink it up!

Yegor Thank you, comrades. I don't usually take alcohol
But I like it when people drink to me –
As they did when I won my People's Award

Semyon This man has won a People's Award
What do you say to that, people?
He is a model fucking postman
And a very handy man with the ladies
Isn't that right, Yegor?

Yegor Well, I'll try to deny it, Semyon Semyonovich

Semyon You wouldn't be believed

Viktor (*coming from the shadows*) You are Semyon Semyonovich?

Semyon is startled. He cries out.

May I shake your hand?

He shakes Semyon's hand. Semyon is looking at him as if he is a ghost.

Yegor This man was on the doorstep, looking for you

Viktor (*with a black look at Alexander*) I had been promised a meeting and I was worried that the sands of time would run out before we'd had a chance to speak

Semyon Who are you? What do you want?

Viktor I'm Viktor Viktorovich. You might have heard of me; I've been published in seven different publications. I'm the people's poet

Kleopatra The people's pest

Viktor Kiki

Kleopatra The people's pipsqueak

Viktor You must be here looking for a new victim

Semyon She's my guest; the only woman who cares two kopeks for me

Serafima I care

Kleopatra Be warned, Semyon Semyonovich

Viktor Yes, be warned

Kleopatra Viktor Viktorovich is not a true poet. He loves only the body and not the soul

Viktor May I speak? (*To Semyon*) Comrade, in my humble career as a highly regarded, controversial writer, I've written extensively about the character of the Russian: so resilient, so often called upon to endure the unendurable. That this character has cracks is deeply moving to me. And I think you embody those cracks

Yegor The character of the Russian has been created by historical materialism. How can it have cracks? It simply *is*

73

Semyon I don't want to offend you or anything, but with you coming in all dressed in black, I thought –

Viktor What?

Semyon Just for a second in the gloom
  I thought I was already dead

Kleopatra Yes, he does look a bit sepulchral,
  A bit grim-reaperish, doesn't he?
  Poor Viktor, you ought to get out in the daylight more

Viktor You know nothing, Kiki, nothing

Kleopatra You're like a poor little wilted plant. You need light

Viktor Semyon Semyonovich
  We artists have become red slaves in the proletariat's harem

Aristarkh You're misquoting

Viktor We sit in the state and we write fanfares
  Drum rolls for the new elite
  Well, I want to be Tolstoy
  Not a drummer
  I would regard it as an honour
  If you would let me write your obituary –
  If it were printed alongside your note
  I guarantee you it would make the strongest statement
  I can craft words
  That will awaken the dullest minds
  Transform the hardest hearts

Aristarkh And tire the keenest intellects

Semyon You can write what you like; I won't be here.
Can I get some more of that booze?

Margarita You'll laugh about this in the morning, love

Semyon I'm laughing now

Yegor I'm fed up reading things about the Russian character, as if we're still peasants painted on a biscuit tin. I'm a postman, right? And I want to read about postmen

Viktor I've written about foundry workers

Yegor Then let the foundry workers read it
I want to read about postmen, do you get it?
The postman's toils
His heavy load, his beating heart

Kleopatra Well that's an audience of one

Yegor There are ten thousand thousand postmen in this Soviet Union, lady. And not one of us has a crack

Aristarkh Ladies and gentlemen –

Yegor And people

Aristarkh We are here to accompany Semyon Semyonovich to . . . dare one say 'the next world' in these secular times?

Yelpidy It is with the profoundest respect that we gather today –

Semyon I'm not dead yet

Aristarkh No, no, my dear friend, we are merely paving the way

Semyon I've got something to ask you, all of you. What is there after?

Aristarkh Well, obviously there's a lavish funeral with invitations to all our premier citizens; graveside orations from myself and other interested parties –

Semyon I don't mean for you, I mean for me

Aristarkh For you?
My dear boy

Semyon Is there life after death? That's what I'm asking. Is there anything out there after this?

Pause.

Aristarkh Well, Father, I rather think this might be one for you

Yelpidy God, I hate that question. I'd rather tell a joke

Alexander Yes, tell a joke

Margarita Let's have a bit of life before death

Yelpidy One night, after a long day's godless theorising, Marx and Hegel decided to go to a knocking shop

Yegor You cannot joke about them

Yelpidy Why not?

Yegor Because communism isn't funny

Alexander I've got a joke. A young man with no money and no prospects decides to end his life –

Semyon I need an answer!

Yelpidy Well, of course there's life after death

Semyon You look as if you want to say 'but'

Yelpidy But
    Well
    You know
    Now
    Your corpse will be water for the great mill of life, that's all we can say. Fill me up there now, Margarita

Margarita It'll make you a lion in the pulpit

Yelpidy And a lamb in your bar

Viktor I'll tell you what your corpse will be

Kleopatra His corpse is not important

Viktor What's important is what will remain

Semyon What will remain?

Viktor The worm
And that is where your power is, Semyon Semyonovich
The worm toils eternally
The worm crawls out and starts to gnaw

Margarita Come on, lads, keep playing

Alexander Let's have a fucking tune

Margarita This is supposed to be a party

The Beggar-Musicians play.

Semyon Wait!
The worm
What does it gnaw on, comrade?

Viktor Let's say it starts with the weakest, with the little
men, the model workers, the Party ants and the splendid
types, those who have never thought, but have a sort of
sadness in them –

Kleopatra Shut up

Viktor The hollow ones, the empty ones. I'm saying this
to comfort you. You will put your worm in them. And
how your worm will multiply

Kleopatra We could get you cremated

Margarita Drink

Aristarkh Dear Semyon, many tempestuous and
passionate young heads will turn towards the path you
are treading. And their fathers will weep without end,
and their mothers will cry over their graves and our great
homeland will start to shake and the gates of the Kremlin

will open wide and our government will come out to us. And we will stand hand in hand, the landowner with the peasant, and – I'm sorry – I didn't cry when my mother died

Alexander So anyway, this young man resolves to top himself
  But he can't decide on a cause

Semyon Are you laughing at me?

Alexander / No

Kleopatra You must try and send us back messages. We could contact you. I could be your vessel. You could move little household objects from place to place

Margarita Drink

Kleopatra Then your influence would continue from beyond the grave. That's the kind of man you are, Semyon; your soul will never die

Semyon You're right
  Drink to me, comrades
  Drink to Semyon, friends
  Drink, you bastards, drink

  The company drinks, shouting Semyon's name.
  Semyon and Alexander start a wild dance. The music
  becomes frenzied. All the others join in.

Aristarkh Semyon Semyonovich, hero of our times. Alone, with a pistol in his hand, he starts out on the great road of Russian history

Viktor Let those who walk this road into the future stumble on his corpse

Yegor To the people

Alexander May you live for ever, mate

*The Beggar-Musicians finish to loud applause and
cheers. Semyon gives them more of his roubles.*

Semyon Take it, lads

Alexander What are you doing? That's ten roubles

Semyon They can have it

Alexander Don't give them your money

Semyon I'm about to die

Alexander Semyon, listen to me. / It's gone far enough

Semyon (*turning from him*) People, listen

Margarita (*to Alexander*) Leave him. He'll come round

Semyon My life is just beginning as it ends

Viktor Speech – he makes a final speech

Semyon I am about to end my life. So who's to blame?
All of them. They do not know that I exist. But I shall get
them on the telephone. I'll phone them and I'll tell them –

Aristarkh Sorry, phone who?

Semyon The Kremlin. I'll telephone the Kremlin and I'll
tell them my name and I'll say openly that I, Semyon
Semyonovich Podsekalnikov, have read Marx and I didn't
think much of him

There are shocked intakes of breath in the room.

I thought he was boring

More shocked intakes of breath.

Then I'll ask to speak to the bloke at the top
    Not just anyone; I'll get the top bloke
    And I'll tell him, telephone to telephone, that he can
    Listen out for when I'm dead
    And when I'm dead I'll say such things –

Shit on fire
How can I say anything?
I haven't written my note

Viktor Dictate it, comrade

Aristarkh Excellent idea. Time is ticking on

Viktor I am poised

Pause.

Semyon You're so good to me, all of you, coming here
I am a man alone and you have shown me that
You care about me, all of you
Look at you
You care about my words, my thoughts
And to my surprise, dear comrades
I find that I am not afraid
My fear has gone
Yes, I'm going to die
And for the first time in my life
I'm completely unafraid
I feel a power growing in me
Like a blaze in my head
There are two hundred million of us
In this Union of Soviets
A huge mass of masses
And I'm the only one
Not cowering in fear
I'm going to die
Hold me down before I start to fly
To think I finally have power
I can do anything, anything
Hold me back
I'm a colossus, I am Caesar
You will see me everywhere
And I'm doing this for us
For all of us

This is me, Semyon, truly me
Shit your pants, you, cowering in the Kremlin
I am the arrow of disillusionment
The meaning of me
Will terrify you
I matter
I matter
I am a boy genius
I am what I always could have been
My life will not insult me
I will not have lived a mockery
Today, tonight, this minute
This second of slippery time
My turn has come
I am
I am

The clock begins to strike twelve. A deathly hush.
Viktor finishes scribbling. Semyon takes Viktor's page.
He signs his name.

Semyon Semyonovich Podsekalnikov

He picks up his gun. He takes his bottle, holding it up
to the company.

Life, I challenge you

He bows. He exits. Silence.
  A round of stunned applause from the company –
apart from Alexander and Margarita.

Yegor He told them to shit their pants
He said it
He told the Kremlin to shit their pants

Kleopatra My love, my beautiful love
I love him, I really do
Look at me, I'm feeling

Alexander (*to Margarita*) I'll follow him

Margarita (*to Alexander*) He won't do it

Viktor 'This second of slippery time'

Aristarkh 'Arrow of disillusionment'

Viktor Can you believe he came out with that?

Margarita Faced with the cold barrel of the gun he won't
be able

Aristarkh This boy; a starving proletarian. What
unexpected quality

Serafima He's not really going to do it, is he?

Yelpidy We should pray

Aristarkh You pray

Yelpidy Father

   Pause.

Yegor Where is it?

Yelpidy What?

Yegor The gunshot

   *Pause. The feeling of discomfort grows until it is
   almost unendurable.*

Aristarkh My brother-in-law
   Has sat in jail
   For five years now

Kleopatra There is another
   Wonderful splendid life
   Somewhere

Serafima What am I feeling? Will somebody tell me what
I'm supposed to be feeling?

Margarita He won't do it

Alexander We are all worthless dogs

Margarita I tell you he won't be able

Serafima He'll walk back in any minute, won't he?

Margarita He'll look back on this when he's an old man

Alexander It's gone far enough

Alexander exits, following Semyon.

Semyon

Pause. We hear a distant gunshot.
  Reactions range from stricken (Serafima) to relieved
(Aristarkh).
  Aristarkh shakily pours himself a glass.

Aristarkh To Semyon Semyonovich Podsekalnikov
He made his choice

Yelpidy May he rest in peace

They drink. Aristarkh brutally smashes his glass.

Act Four

Dawn, growing into a sunny morning. Masha enters.
As well as her belongings, she carries a loaf of bread and
some cheese. There is a figure sleeping in the bed.

Masha Semyon?
    I knew you wouldn't do it
    Just like you knew I wouldn't get on any train
    I've always believed in you
    I walked instead
    I walked and walked
    And at first light a feeling came on me
    Like I was floating inches off the street
    I joined a queue for bread
    It brought me back to earth, the smell of food
    I watched the daylight soak the city
    And I thought about your face
    And thinking of it made me warm.
    We're hungry; that's all that's wrong with us.
    Would you like some bread?

    She gently lifts the sheet. Serafima is lying there in a
    stupor.

Mum! What're you doing in our bed?
    Where's my husband?
    Come on, move it

    Masha roughly shakes her. Serafima moans. The
    remains of the party slowly become apparent to Masha.

What's been going on?
    Mother, where's Semyon?

Serafima I can't bear it
  They're out on the wasteland looking for his body

  The shock hits Masha.

They had to wait for dawn so they could see

  Masha falls to her knees.

Where were you? Why did you go? I came running after
you to try and bring you back but you were gone

Masha Semyon
  Semyon
  No

Serafima I'm sorry
  It's like a bad old dream
  I'm sorry, Masha

  *Serafima takes Masha in her arms. They hold each
  other. Enter Yelpidy, Aristarkh and Viktor.*

Yelpidy Weep, weep, young widow. Hold your little ones
close and weep, weep for their daddy

Aristarkh What daddy?

Yelpidy The little ones' daddy

Aristarkh What little ones?

Yelpidy His little ones

Aristarkh There are no little ones

Yelpidy Well, that's fate then; he missed his chance.
Weep, young widow, for the little ones he never had

Aristarkh Thank you, Father, for those comforting words
from the Church. My dear young widow, it is true. Your
husband is dead

Viktor And yet he lives. His image is shining with life.
The departed Semyon Semyonovich lives on in our midst

as a poetic symbol of our disenchanted times. And as this symbol, he will never die

Masha emits a terrible cry of grief.

Aristarkh Goodness me

Serafima Where did you find him?

Aristarkh Under a tree

Serafima Is he a mess?

Aristarkh From compassion, I couldn't look

Serafima Where's the body?

Aristarkh Those endowed with strength of arm are bringing him. We are the advance party. Madam, we have little time to lose. The corpse must be prepared

Masha emits another terrible cry of grief.

Heavens above

Viktor He died an honourable death. You should be proud

Aristarkh His funeral will be inspired by that of Lenin himself. Obviously we don't have the same budget, but Semyon Semyonovich deserves nothing less

Masha DEAD
HE IS DEAD

Serafima Masha
Masha

Viktor Honour and glory to the wife of our dearly departed

Aristarkh Widow, stand with your head held high. He died a hero

Masha MY LIFE IS OVER

Aristarkh Come on now
You do understand what he was doing?

Masha SENYECHKA

Yelpidy Why do women always make this racket?
Time, I'd say, to beat a quick retreat
We'll come back when she's in the stupor that comes
next
Then the mother might be in the mood for making tea

Viktor Wait – he comes. Our fallen comrade

*They stand back respectfully. Alexander, Yegor and the
Beggar-Musicians enter, carrying Semyon's body.
Margarita and Kleopatra follow behind. Semyon has
a wound to the head. The sight of him horrifies Masha
into silence.*
Yelpidy starts to pray.

Yelpidy Soul of Christ, sanctify him
Body of Christ, save him

Alexander and Yegor lay Semyon on the bed.

Blood of Christ, inebriate him
Water from the side of Christ, wash him
Passion of Christ, strengthen him

Alexander Masha
I'm sorry
I ran after him too late
Masha
I'm sorry

Alexander goes up to his room and shuts the door.

Yelpidy Oh good Jesus, hear us
Hide this man within thy wounds
Defend him from the wicked enemy

Kleopatra People followed us / asking who he was. I –

Margarita Shut it, can't you?

Yelpidy Call him at the hour of his death
And bid him come to Thee
That he may give Thee praise for all eternity, Amen

All Amen

Kleopatra I told the bystanders what Semyon had done
and why
They were deeply moved
And now a crowd is gathering outside

Yegor Maria Lukianovna
He was curled up on the wasteland
Eyes closed in peace
I've brought you back his gun

Masha I'll kill myself

Margarita No you won't

Yegor I didn't know Semyon Semyonovich that well –
not until the day he died. In fact, I thought him lazy –
and a yob

Aristarkh This man is one of life's natural fools

Yegor As you know, I am a model worker; recipient of
a People's Award for speed and diligence. But Semyon
Semyonovich put into words thoughts so secret I would
never have dared think them. If those in the Kremlin
could have heard, they would indeed have shat
themselves –

Serafima Yegor Timoveivich, now is not the time

Yegor There are hundreds of men like him, with secret
thoughts locked in their breasts

Masha Go away

Yegor He called himself a boy genius. That's true of all
of us

88

Aristarkh Another time, comrade

Yegor This humble postman asks if there is anything that he might do

Masha No

Yegor I would lay myself down flat
In your dear service.
If you would let me kiss your hand

Masha Fuck off

Yegor Thank you

Masha All of you, fuck off
Get out of here
I hate you

Yegor makes his way upstairs.

Yelpidy I think it's time we took our leave

Masha I want to die
I want to die

Upstairs, Yegor quietly exits.

Kleopatra (*to Viktor*) That girl is devastated, is she not?

Viktor She is indeed

Kleopatra Semyon Semyonovich inspired love. Even his domestics loved him

Serafima Father, how will we bury him?
We've not a kopeck to our names

Aristarkh Good woman. Do not fear. We have taken it upon ourselves to pay for everything

Yelpidy With the generosity of the Church

Aristarkh And the last of my mother's bone china, we're providing top quality undertakers, wreaths

Yelpidy Sung mass with a full choir

Viktor The poem I'm composing, for which I'll take no fee

Aristarkh A camera, a new suit of clothes for him to wear

Kleopatra And something for you women, too. I'm sure he'd want you in his retinue – however poor and humble you may be

Masha Get out

Yelpidy I'll go and book the choir

Yelpidy exits.

Kleopatra You shall have a hand-made hat, perhaps the latest thing in felt, something elegant to lift your features

Serafima That's lovely; what a lovely girl you are

Kleopatra exits.

Aristarkh I took the liberty of ordering his coffin yesterday. It's made of oak, with fittings in a modernist style; quite the finest

Serafima Thank you, sir. It's wonderful that Semyon's getting all that, but can I put in a request for the living?

Viktor The living?

Serafima We haven't got any food

Aristarkh Food

Viktor We must start a fund

Serafima A fund

Aristarkh Of course; a fund

Viktor I'll see to it myself

Aristarkh We shall return before you know it

Viktor and Aristarkh exit.

Serafima What lovely, educated men; so clean

Margarita A fund? You don't miss a trick, you

Serafima You look after her while I wash the carcass.
He's going to be on show. We don't want him dirtying his
coffin. I'll work like a machine on him

Margarita (*to Masha*) You poor love

Serafima (*examining the body*) Now, I saw a lot of head
wounds in the war
   At this close range the brains would usually slide out
   With little bits of skull lodged in the mess.
   That's very neat
   Just a little hole above the ear

   *Serafima climbs up to the bathroom. We hear her
   filling a bucket of water.*

Masha Put me with Semyon
   I want to hold him

Margarita I never thought he'd do it
   I can't believe he did

Masha I want to die with him

Margarita No you don't

Masha I want to die

Margarita Masha
   I'm so sorry

   *Margarita puts Masha next to Semyon. Serafima is
   coming down the stairs with a bucket and cloth.*

Serafima Everything taken care of
   A fund for our expenses
   A decadent hat

Margarita You're like your mother. You'd survive an
Arctic storm

Serafima On every cloud a silver lining
  We'll be all right, my girl
  His death will give us life
  I wish we had a clean dishcloth; never mind
  (*To Margarita.*) Roll your silky sleeves up then

Margarita I'm no good with corpses
  My vocation's always been with men who are alive

  She climbs the stairs.

Alexander needs me

Serafima You know, for all your fancy business talk,
you're still a fool

Margarita I know. But I've never seen him look like that

Serafima Like what?

Margarita Seems Kalabushkin's got a heart
  Beating somewhere, after all

  *Margarita knocks on Alexander's door. Alexander
  takes her into his room. He shuts the door on their
  emotional embrace. Masha is clinging to Semyon.*

Masha He always kept me warm and now he's cold

  *Masha kisses Semyon. She is bewildered. She looks
  round at Serafima.*

But not that cold

  *She sits up. She pokes him. Semyon suddenly snores
  loudly.*

Bastard

  *She makes her hands into a single fist and hits him in
  the heart. Semyon starts.*

Semyon Dead
I'm dead
Hosanna
The pain
I'm flying

Masha Semyon Semyonovich

Semyon Angel, I hear you
Take me to God
The light hurts me
Hosanna

Masha slaps him round the face.

Masha Wake up

Semyon Pain
I'm dead
Am I in hell?

Serafima You're here

Semyon Dear Father, I have suffered down on Earth;
don't make me suffer more

Serafima Semyon, I'm not your father; I'm your mother-
in-law

Semyon Serafima
Where are we?
Are you dead too?
Am I with you for ever?
This is awful
This is hell

Masha hits and punches him as she speaks.

Masha Wake up, you idiot
You're not dead; you're drunk
You're stinking of it
You bastard

93

How dare you
I thought you'd gone

Semyon Masha
Am I alive?

Masha Yes

Semyon I'm alive

She hits him again.

Mashenka, I'm alive

*Masha starts to cry. Semyon holds her. Serafima
wearily picks up the bucket.*

Serafima Well, we'll not be needing this. You can wash
yourself

She starts back up the stairs.

Semyon I'm alive

*We hear the sound of Margarita and Alexander
making love.*

Serafima They've no respect for the dead

She locks herself in the toilet.

Semyon I left here with my gun. I saw a beggar on a
trolley by the wasteland. He had no fingers and no legs.
He couldn't see me; both his eyes were white. I gave him
all my money. He gripped it pincer-like, thumb against
his ruined hand. I said: 'Take it, brother. Ten roubles for
you there.' 'Don't insult me with your litter, curse you,'
he replied and he let it fly away. I saw it sail up through
the street light and the ground started shifting like thin
ice. I ran. I stumbled over clumps of grass and wire and
frozen shit. I didn't stop until I hit a tree. I knew the
place; the tree that blossoms during May and for a
fortnight every year looks like a piece of heaven; but last

94

night it was freezing barren black. I held the trunk with one hand and I put the gun end in my mouth. Turns out it was the bottle so I drank until the stars all burst and everything went dark. Then my fingers closed round metal and I brought it up to see, and bang –

Margarita and Alexander finish.

Masha You missed

Semyon Reckon I did

Masha You stupid twat

Semyon Can't even kill myself

Masha Useless, you

Semyon (*putting his hand up to his wound*) Look at that. I got a wound, though

Masha You were miles out

Semyon Nice to know you're glad to see me, anyway

Masha Well. Better luck next time, eh?

Semyon Mashenka

Masha Am I really so horrible to live with?

Semyon No
 I am

Masha Senya
 Senyechka

Serafima emerges from the toilet.

Serafima Jesus of Nazareth, save us or we perish!
 What'll we tell those people?
 They've gone to plan your funeral

Masha So they have

Serafima They're modelling it on Lenin's

Semyon Shit on fire

Serafima We'll take care of all the bills, they said

Semyon Your husband died a symbol

Serafima They're even making me a hat

Semyon I'm supposed to be dead

> *Two undertakers, Stepan Vasilievich and Oleg*
> *Leonidovich, enter. They are carrying a coffin and*
> *some wreaths.*

Oleg Is this where the dead man lives?

Semyon What?

Oleg The dead man. Does he live here?

Stepan To you, Oleg, to you

Oleg Mind that thing; hang on

Semyon Who are you?

Stepan We've come from 'Eternity'

Masha Pardon?

Stepan From 'Eternity'

Oleg You know, the funeral parlour

Stepan Right, where do you want it?

Oleg Come on please, comrades; it's heavy. We've carried
it all the way from the workshop

> *Pause. Semyon, Masha and Serafima are staring at*
> *them in horror.*

Stepan Look, I know it's a bit of a shock when you first
see it, but please take comfort from the fact that it's the
very best one we do

Oleg Fantastic coffin, this. I'd have one myself if I could afford it – and if I was dead, obviously

Stepan Oh Jesus, let's just put it down

Stepan and Oleg put the coffin on the table.

Right, where's the incoming occupant?

Semyon What?

Stepan The incoming occupant. You see they make us say that, as if obscure language makes losing your loved one easier or something. But that's 'Eternity' for you: full of obscurity. I say, why don't we just say 'the body'?

Oleg The corpse. Where's the corpse?

Stepan What's its name?

Oleg (*consulting a clipboard*) Semyon Semyonovich Podsekalnikov

Semyon Here

Oleg Where?

Serafima He's not ready yet. We haven't finished him

Stepan We're supposed to lift him in for you

Semyon No thanks

Stepan It's part of the service. We're meant to do it

Oleg Once the *mortis* sets in, it's a tricky job

Serafima We'll manage

Oleg It's upsetting, love. They don't bend

Masha We'll look after him ourselves, thank you

Serafima We like a challenge

Stepan You sure?

Masha Yes, thanks

Oleg Right, then

He hands Semyon a clipboard.

Sign for it, will you?

Semyon takes up the pen. He falters.

Semyon Feels weird. You do it

He hands the clipboard to Masha. She signs.

Oleg And there for the wreaths, please

She signs again.

Stepan There's a lot of folk out there; quite a crowd. Was he well known?

Semyon Not really

Stepan Must have been a Party member, or something. What was he, a People's Commissar?

Semyon He was just a
Nothing, really

Oleg Well, top-class coffin, that. I hope he gets good use of it

Serafima Thanks, lads. Cheerio then

Stepan I feel great compassion for the bereaved

Oleg So do I

Stepan I always pity the dead person too

Semyon Thank you

Pause.

Oleg Glad you like the coffin, then

Stepan Have you got any change?

Masha comes forward rummaging in her pockets. She finds a tiny coin.

Masha Good luck

Stepan and Oleg leave, insulted. Masha picks up one of the wreaths. She reads the dedication.

'For my beloved Semyon. A fighter, a hero and an unforgettable son-in-law.' (*She looks at Serafima.*) It's from you

Serafima Did I write that?

Masha No, they did

Serafima We haven't got a body

Masha What are we going to do?

We hear the front door opening.

Serafima It's them

Semyon I've let them down. They trusted me. They were banking on me

We hear Aristarkh off, speaking through a loudhailer.

Aristarkh (*off*) Comrades, this humble dwelling holds all that remains of Semyon Semyonovich Podsekalnikov

Semyon They're the only people who've ever had time for anything I've said

Aristarkh (*off*) In a few moments we shall escort him to his final resting place

Semyon I thought I was a maggot. They made me feel a man

Yelpidy (*off*) St Josef's on Zverkov Street, where you are welcome to reacquaint yourselves with God

Semyon Look at that thing. It's fit for a prince

Aristarkh (*off*) Await us here, comrades. We shall soon emerge with your fallen brother

Masha We'll tell them the truth. How hard can that be? We'll tell them you're alive

Serafima They were going to start a fund for us, a fund, Semyon

Semyon My death would have provided for you?

Serafima We were going to have an income

Semyon Where's my gun? I'll kill myself

Masha I've got a better idea – I'll kill you

Serafima You won't have to; they'll kill him
Holy Virgin, pray for us

*Aristarkh, Yelpidy and Viktor come up the stairs.
Masha and Serafima turn to face them. Behind
them, Semyon panics.
He jumps into the coffin and lies there, as if dead.*

Aristarkh My dear young widow, the crowd is growing, swelling, multiplying beyond our wildest expectations

Masha There's been a terrible mistake

Yelpidy I have preached the parable of / Podsekalnikov

Aristarkh We have all addressed the crowd, some more / reasonably than others

Viktor I've managed to compose his praises in this verse

Masha It's a mistake

Aristarkh I've also contacted the press. / His fame will spread

Viktor Revered widow, here is our collective effort to replace your husband. It's just the beginning

He hands her a collection of money.

Masha We can't take this

Serafima Holy Jesus, I can't bear it

Masha Thank you but
He isn't dead
It's a mistake
He's still alive

Pause.

Aristarkh Well, I'm rather confused that you should say that, my dear

Masha We thought he was dead
And so did he, actually
But as you can see –

Masha turns. She sees Semyon, corpse-like in the coffin.

Serafima Has he died?

Masha Semyon
What are you doing?
Get up out of there

Aristarkh Oh no, she's hysterical

Yelpidy (*going to Semyon*) Look at him. Dead

Masha Semyon
GET UP I SAID
He's alive

Aristarkh My dear widow –

Masha I'm not a widow; he's alive

Viktor She's trapped in her moment of nemesis
Unable to face her tragic hubris

Aristarkh Stop it

Masha Mother, tell them

Serafima (*taking the money from Masha*) Masha, when you see it from their point of view –

Yelpidy I've seen this happen before. She'll either come round in an hour or two or she's a case for the asylum

Viktor Tragedy

Alexander and Margarita appear on the landing.

Masha Semyon, I'm warning you. Get up or I'll murder you

She goes to shake him. Yelpidy and Aristarkh stop her.

Yelpidy (*stopping her*) Widow, do not defile the dead

Aristarkh We can't let you do it

Masha Semyon

Viktor You must face the truth

Masha Get up, you idiot
You're making it harder for yourself

Yelpidy Your husband is dead

Masha Semyon

Alexander What's going on?

Masha Alexander Kalabushkin, Semyon is alive

Margarita Oh no; poor girl

Alexander Mashenka

Margarita I once had a neighbour who kept his dead mother sitting at the table for sixteen days because he couldn't believe she'd gone. It was the smell that convinced him in the end

Masha He was talking to me five minutes ago

Serafima (*hiding the money in her apron*) You know, Masha, you never can tell with these head wounds.

I remember the bone surgeon telling me that a fellow can be up and walking around one minute with blood gushing out of his ear, telling you a fine old joke and next minute – gone

Masha What are you saying?

Serafima I'm saying brain explosion. Look at him

Masha Alexander Kalabushkin, he's not dead

Yelpidy She needs rest
  Seclusion in a dark place
  Possibly restraints

Alexander Masha, I carried him home. He was frozen to the touch

Masha Well, he thawed

Aristarkh Is there a dark room where she can get some rest?

Margarita Bring her up here

Alexander Come on, Masha

Masha You wouldn't. Alexander Kalabushkin, you couldn't –

Alexander I'm sorry, Mashenka
  I'm so sorry
  But you'll thank me for it, love

  Alexander puts Masha over his shoulder. He carries her up the stairs.

Masha Semyon Semyonovich Podsekalnikov, I will get you for this. You toe-rag. You coward. Why is life so difficult to face?

Margarita Come on, girl

Masha Let me go
  Put me down

Alexander I'm sorry

Margarita Leave her with me

Masha All right, all right, he's dead
  I believe you
  Just don't bury him
  Don't bury him

  *Semyon sits up in a panic. No one is looking at the
  coffin; all their eyes are on Masha. She is the only
  person who notices Semyon.*

Semyon, you FOOL

  Margarita closes the door. Semyon hurriedly lies down.

Viktor Her grief is epic
  Cassandra tormented
  Andromache at the gates of Troy

Aristarkh She nearly bit me. (*Setting up the camera.*)
Now, without wishing to ride roughshod over the needs
of the bereaved, I'd like to point out that the crowd
should not be kept waiting. They have come to see a
suicide and suicide they'll have. (*To Viktor.*) Have you
sent his final words to the printer?

Viktor Of course

Aristarkh With the changes I suggested?

Viktor Yes

Yelpidy One has to admit that this dead man is not the
finest choice

Alexander What do you mean?

Yelpidy Well, it's a pity that a People's Commissar or a
society figure hadn't decided to shoot himself in the head

Aristarkh I disagree – his obscurity is his perfection

Yelpidy How?

Aristarkh Because we can mould him. In our careful hands, he will become the model dead man

Viktor You're right. We can construct a truth. Listen to my poem; I've chosen a folksy, populist style so it will appeal to the masses. We need them to recognise themselves

Aristarkh (*to Serafima*) Madam, could we have you by the coffin?

Serafima Here?

Aristarkh And you, Alexander Kalabushkin; you've got a good face. Stand there

Alexander No thanks

Alexander moves away. We hear a plaintive melody, coming closer.

Viktor
A young working man, without job or means
Found his life was a series of frustrated dreams.
But the path he was given he chose not to tread.
For society's sake, he chose death instead.

Aristarkh (*to Serafima*) Madam, forgive me, but I don't think a smile is appropriate

The photograph is taken.

Viktor
When we climb up snowdrifts or lie in the grass,
Betraying his pain with our carefree hearts
Let us think of that second of slippery time.
When death drew him forwards at midnight's slow chime,
His body now crumpled, the gun in his hand,
They killed him – the philistines – no more could he stand!

Aristarkh Doesn't scan

Viktor It's for the peasants, you pedant

*Kleopatra enters followed by the Beggar-Musicians,
who are playing the plaintive melody. She speaks over
the last verse of Viktor's poem.*

His coffin will / lead us through life from this day

Kleopatra The crowd is enormous. We had to fight / our
way through

Viktor
    The ultimate price he paid, I would say,
    / Our hopes are now with him buried below.

Kleopatra I told them, 'I am a murderer!'

Viktor Kiki, I'm reciting!

Kleopatra Semyon Semyonovich wanted me body and
soul and when I said, 'No, my darling!' he ended his life.
I murdered him

Viktor Murdered him? You?

Kleopatra Yes, you drummer

Viktor Your body is made entirely of lies

Kleopatra My body is HIS! They've been so moved by
our tragedy

*Masha comes out onto the landing. Margarita follows
her.*

Viktor By your what?

Kleopatra By the tragedy of our great love

Viktor That's quick work, even for you. You only knew
him a day

Kleopatra It was long enough. He took his life because
of me. If only you were man enough to do the same

Viktor Oh, if only

Kleopatra Ah, you have a camera –
Let me throw myself upon him

Masha (*running down the stairs*) Over my dead body

Yelpidy Why do these women insist on hurling themselves
at corpses?

Masha and Kleopatra meet over the coffin.

Masha He's mine, you stupid, stuck-up tart

Kleopatra How dare you, you cleaner

Masha I'm his wife

Kleopatra You're quite mistaken

Masha No, I'm not

Margarita She's his wife

Kleopatra Well, what does it matter? He wanted me, me

Masha Semyon, sort this out

Kleopatra He died for my love

Masha He will in a minute

The men restrain Masha and Kleopatra.

Aristarkh Ladies, please, this is not a personal drama.
Semyon Semyonovich died so that others could act for
him. / His death is a clarion call to Russia's intellectuals

Viktor He had a poet's sensibility. He died because the
state had no faith / in him

Yelpidy He died because he had no faith. / Perilous is the
godless path he trod

Margarita He died because he'd had a row with Masha /
and he thought she'd left him

Alexander He died because he didn't have a fucking job / and it sent him twisted

Masha HE ISN'T DEAD

Pause.

Serafima Is that my hat?

Kleopatra Yes

Serafima (*taking it*) Thank you so much

Aristarkh Gentlemen – and people – there is no reason why Semyon Semyonovich could not be poet and lover, political thinker, unemployed worker, religious devotee – and immortal to those who loved him. Our model dead man could be all of these things

Viktor You're right

Yelpidy I'll put the lid on, shall I?

Alexander I'll put the lid on –
When his wife is ready
Masha?

Masha You take him. Put him on show and then shove him in the ground. God help you, Semyon

Alexander picks up the lid. He raises it over the coffin.

Alexander I was no friend to you
Forgive me

Semyon embraces Alexander.

Semyon No, no, you forgive me

Aristarkh screams. There is pandemonium.

Forgive me, comrades. All of you, forgive me

Yelpidy Get thee from me

Kleopatra The living dead

Aristarkh Get back! Get back!

Serafima It's a miracle! A resurrection, look!

Semyon I can't go on. Sorry, but I've got to live

Viktor Alive?

Semyon Yes

Masha I tried to tell you

Aristarkh You were supposed to kill yourself

Semyon I tried to

Serafima He only missed by an inch

Margarita We wept for you

Alexander Actually, I just got dust in my eyes

Masha Semyon

Semyon I'm sorry

Kleopatra I have wasted my suffering

Viktor You Judas

Aristarkh You have put your own interests before society

Semyon Society? What's that? As far as I can tell from you it's a factory of slogans. My society is here, with her, and her, and them

Aristarkh I thought you were a hero and I find you are a worm. How can you go on living?

Semyon I don't know; thoughtlessly
Like a chicken with its head cut off perhaps.
I don't want to die. Not for you, not for them, not for clever men or the masses, not for romance, not for art, and not for God

Yelpidy Blasphemer

Viktor We were going to make you a symbol

Semyon You could have made me a bearded lady
  What would I care in that box?
  I am alive and well
  And nothing on this Earth has ever scared me
  Like the thought of lying there for ever
  With the lid nailed down

Yelpidy He has made fools of us all

Masha I tried to tell you

Viktor Are you laughing at our expense?

Aristarkh Our literal expense. My mother's china

Kleopatra Semyon, you lied

Semyon I didn't lie. I meant to do it
  But I can't be your model dead man
  I can't set the world ablaze
  I'm not a multiplying worm
  All I want is a quiet life and a decent wage

Viktor That's bourgeois

Aristarkh Listen to him

Viktor Everything he says is counter-revolutionary

Aristarkh You're right

Viktor Why didn't we realise before? He's a traitor to the revolution

Semyon What have I ever done against the revolution?

Aristarkh You spoke

Semyon You all wanted me to speak

Aristarkh But only as a dead man. I told you from the start that there are things the living cannot say – and you have said them, boy

Semyon Then let me whisper
Let me sometimes whisper, 'It's a hard life,' 'It's a hard life.'
Because we need to, people like me with not enough bread.
Leave me free to whisper
You're so busy constructing truth I doubt you'll even hear

The noise of the crowd is growing louder; funereal hymns are being sung.

Kleopatra Listen

Viktor The crowd

Yelpidy We have promised them a suicide

Aristarkh And we cannot deliver

Semyon It's a hard life

Kleopatra Viktor, what'll we do?

Viktor Kiki

Semyon It's a hard life

Yelpidy The merciless masses

Viktor They'll tear us apart

Kleopatra Save me from the crowd

Kleopatra throws herself upon Viktor.

Viktor My perfect muse

Aristarkh You have exposed us to the rage and ridicule of all those people
You cheat, you thief, you utter nonentity
You have dug us a grave with your own hands
And you dare to survive?

Yelpidy We must have a body

Kleopatra Shoot him

Masha Shoot her

Aristarkh Recant and shoot yourself

Yelpidy I could get him with this shovel if you held him down

Semyon No need; I've still a bullet left
Take the gun, comrades
If I've committed any crime
If I've brought death or misfortune to a single soul
Then take your shot

Aristarkh Huh

Semyon Come forward, Aristarkh Dominikovich Grand-Skubik. If you can name my crime, then take the gun and shoot me

Serafima is hiding the money. Aristarkh takes the gun. He aims it at Semyon.

Aristarkh You wasted our money

Semyon I'll pay your money back, every kopek

Masha I'll work for you. I'll slave for you

Serafima I could work down the mines; in the sewers. I'll take on anything

Masha We'll go begging, all of us

Aristarkh You wasted our time

Margarita is at the top of the stairs. She lifts Serafima's bucket and holds it over the heads of Aristarkh, Viktor, Yelpidy and Kleopatra.

Margarita Anyone thinking of firing that gun should know that I have a bucket of slops up here, from the toilet of this slum. He who moves, gets it

Aristarkh lowers the gun.

Aristarkh I wasn't going to fire. How could you think that? I'm a civilised man. I just wanted to teach him a lesson

Margarita Take it off him, Masha

Masha takes the gun and aims it at them.

Kleopatra (*trying to hide herself in his jacket*) Viktor, shelter me

Masha Get back

Yelpidy I'm a / humble man of God

Viktor We're peace-loving artists, men of the people
  We believe in / humane socialism

Aristarkh We always put the / proletariat first

Kleopatra Spare me

Masha Shut it, tart

Margarita Semyon, get out of that coffin. Kalabushkin, put the lid on it

Semyon and Alexander obey her commands.

Viktor Kiki, you smell like a meadow

Kleopatra I belong in your jacket

Margarita Right, there's your body
  There's your hollow truth
  Take it and go

Aristarkh But it's empty

Alexander Who's to know?

Margarita Tell them he shot his head off and you can't show the corpse. Now pick it up

Alexander You heard the lady

Viktor Come on, Kiki. We'll get through this

Kleopatra I can't
I'm too sensitive

Serafima Chuck the slops on her

Kleopatra moves with a squeal and takes her place as pallbearer.

Margarita And if any of you ever bother this man or his family again, I'll tell the world that coffin's empty and I'll ban you from my bar

Kleopatra / No

Yelpidy Margarita, / you couldn't. I'm just a lamb

Aristarkh Dear lady, it's my / window on the world

Viktor No, please. We're all friends here. All civilised friends

Alexander Play them out, lads

The Beggar-Musicians play an inappropriate tune.

Semyon (*waving them off*) Good luck with the funeral
Hope they like your poem

*The four pallbearers leave with their coffin.
The remaining five celebrate.*

Masha Thank you

Alexander You've really got style, Margarita.
A bucket of shite?

Margarita It's only water

Alexander Beautiful
Beautiful

Serafima Look at them go
The crowd parting like the Red Sea
Their heads bowed in respect.
Amazing what people will believe

Margarita I'll open a bottle, shall I?

Alexander Music to my ears

She goes into Alexander's room.

Masha Alexander, go and fetch Yegor –
Tell him what's happened.
Let him come and share

Alexander goes up the stairs.

I told him to fuck off when I thought you were dead
I was horrible to him

Semyon I am in love
I'm in love with my hands, with my feet, with my legs
With this bed
With my wife
With the hawthorn tree
And the blue sky
With that crowd
With the music
And more than anything, I have fallen in love with my stomach
My poor stomach
It was all I could think of in that coffin

Masha Senyechka, I got bread

Semyon I haven't eaten for a whole day
And a night and another endless day
Not since that black pudding
Mashenka
You best of all wives
I am wildly in love with that bread

Masha Let me furnish you, Semyon

Serafima You can eat the lot. Here, we can afford plenty more. Five thousand loaves

She puts the collection of money on the table. Margarita uncorks a bottle.

Margarita You can afford some glasses, too

Masha Mother, we have to give that back

Serafima How can we? It's Semyon's. He earned it by dying

Alexander comes out of the attic. He is ashen.

Margarita What is it?

A hush falls.

Alexander, what's happened?

Alexander Yegor Timoveivich
Yegor has hanged himself

Serafima Holy God, why?

Silence.

Alexander He left us a note

Semyon What does it say?

Alexander 'Semyon is right. Why live?'

The End.